SoulMate Map©

Find Yourself, Find Your Match!
A Blueprint to Authentic Love

A Workbook of Self Discovery

Revealing a New Reality About You and Love

Written by: Relationship Educator ♥ Denise Culley

Printed in the United States of America

First Printing, 11/2011
Second Printing, revision and new cover, 4/2016

Author: Denise Culley
Cover design by Michelle Ivanovich

ISBN 978-0-9840188-0-2

Self Published by:
Relationships123 Publishing
P.O. Box 3386
Paradise, CA 95967

To contact Denise Culley directly:
denise@soulmateplan.com

To place direct orders, contact
customerservice@soulmateplan.com

Website: http://SoulMatePlan.com

Order paperback versions from Amazon
(use either links below)

http://goo.gl/jiMWro

http://amazon.com/Soulmate-Map-Denise-Culley/dp/0984018808

This book is also available for Kindle, Nook and iBook

Acknowledgments

First, I would like to thank the many wonderful women who have inspired me to write this book. They are the ones I coach weekly, and they will remain nameless to respect their privacy. You know who you are! Yes, YOU!

Your openness and willingness to explore new ideas are both heartwarming and inspirational to me, as is your courage and steadfast determination to never give up on yourselves and never give up on love, even through the most difficult times! You deserve nothing less than the relationship of your dreams. You provided me with all the ongoing encouragement I needed to move forward with this project.

I am eternally grateful to my husband. You are my partner, my greatest cheerleader and the love of my life. Thank God I did so much work before meeting you, so that I was ready for our relationship. The journey we share together is a life I love. Your faith in me and your constant acknowledgment and partnership are not only a great model for others (you know all my women friends and clients want an Emmett of their own), but are also a validation of the model for love and partnership that we believe in.

I love you in all ways and always!

To my editor and wordsmith artiste:

Your style of editing and your support has provided me with unbridled freedom. The greatest gift that you gave me was the freedom to write and not have to worry about writing style, grammar or syntax. I could just write! The words could pour out of me as freely as if I was speaking to a client. I hope you know how invaluable you have been to me, and you have become a real friend. I don't think this experience would have been as enjoyable, nor could I have been so fully self-expressed, had I not known you would be there in the background, ensuring the words conveyed my meaning, were fun to read, as well as inspirational. Every time I look at this book, I will think of you! I wish you a lifetime of happiness and growth!

I want *you all* to know, you inspired me to write! That too was a surprising gift.

Denise

Table of Contents

SoulMate Map

Find Yourself, Find Your Match!
How to Recognize Authentic Love

Acknowledgments

First, I would like to thank the many wonderful women who have inspired me to write this book. They are the ones I coach weekly, and they will remain nameless to respect their privacy. You know who you are! Yes, YOU!

Your openness and willingness to explore new ideas are both heartwarming and inspirational to me, as is your courage and steadfast determination to never give up on yourselves and never give up on love, even through the most difficult times! You deserve nothing less than the relationship of your dreams. You provided me with all the ongoing encouragement I needed to move forward with this project.

I am eternally grateful to my husband. You are my partner, my greatest cheerleader and the love of my life. Thank God I did so much work before meeting you, so that I was ready for our relationship. The journey we share together is a life I love. Your faith in me and your constant acknowledgment and partnership are not only a great model for others (you know all my women friends and clients want an Emmett of their own), but are also a validation of the model for love and partnership that we believe in.

I love you in all ways and always!

To my editor and wordsmith artiste:

Your style of editing and your support has provided me with unbridled freedom. The greatest gift that you gave me was the freedom to write and not have to worry about writing style, grammar or syntax. I could just write! The words could pour out of me as freely as if I was speaking to a client. I hope you know how invaluable you have been to me, and you have become a real friend. I don't think this experience would have been as enjoyable, nor could I have been so fully self-expressed, had I not known you would be there in the background, ensuring the words conveyed my meaning, were fun to read, as well as inspirational. Every time I look at this book, I will think of you! I wish you a lifetime of happiness and growth!

I want *you all* to know, you inspired me to write! That too was a surprising gift.

Denise

Forward

This book was inspired by the women I have coached, including some that were single and some that were in relationships. All of them shared the need for clarity. They weren't aware of their full potential to find a great and healthy love. They also didn't know how to understand or handle their men. Many single women had given up on love, or they were repeating the same broken patterns, or wasting time on men that were obviously not into them.

The women that really embraced their new partnership model blossomed as they raised their standards and began to see men from a whole new perspective. They ventured into their new roles as relationship goddesses, and as a result, their lives were transformed with the joy of authentic love.

Seeing all of this taking place was awe inspiring. So much so, that I felt a desire to share these simple to learn tools that I have developed and used with my single clients and women contemplating separation or divorce. To my great surprise, the knowledge that had been culminating for so many years just flowed out of me. I knew the translation was a success when my editor transformed her relationship as she worked on the book.

The idea of transforming women's lives and empowering them to truly discover themselves is my greatest life purpose. Some of you may already know that my husband and I offered weekend workshops devoted to transforming people's partnership models. That experience was moving beyond tears. I witnessed first-hand the growth and enlightenment of both men and women as they were inspired by new possibilities and new tools for love and partnership.

Knowing that this wisdom has been successfully funneled into these pages is more deeply fulfilling to me than I can express. The same level of transformation we achieved in our workshops can now be experienced through the reading and homework lessons ahead. It was designed as a step-by-step manual to create a map to your soul mate, that is specifically tailored to you, and it was also designed to help you find him!

My greatest hope is that the lessons in this book reach hundreds of thousands of women, and the landscape of relationships is changed forever until divorce becomes nothing but a small and insignificant statistic.

Enough reveling in hopes and dreams from me!

I wanted to include the Editor's testimonial, after learning how working on this book actually impacted her life. When you hire an editor, you are naturally hiring them to correct your typos and grammar and to keep the pace of the book interesting and entertaining. I never considered for a moment that her own experience with this book would have a profound impact on her life as well. She was already in a relationship when she began work on this project, and wasn't actively looking for help with the difficulties she was having with her partner. By learning these lessons as she worked, she just learned how to "be" in a way that inspired him to alter his perception of how to "behave" in a relationship, and now he has really stepped up to be everything she did not know she could ask for! I thought it was so inspiring that I asked her to write something about it. Here are *her* words, *her* experience:

Editor's Testimonial:

The request was simple. Polish the clarity and vibrancy of the writing quality in the SoulMate Map©. The result? I was being paid to have my relationship questions answered! I think I have a pretty good head on my shoulders, but love and relationships take you to confusing places, where sometimes you don't know which way is up, much less how to make the best decisions. It's not like life has a rule-book out there to tell you where to draw a line or where to compromise. The SoulMate Map© turned out to be the guide I never knew I always needed. And that was before I decided to actually do the homework and exercises myself. The truth is, I have always shrugged off anything that could fall in the remote vicinity of "self-help" but now, I count my lucky stars for tumbling face first into this wisdom! The SoulMate Map© has been a wonderfully enlightening experience that has not only taught me to understand men, but how to understand myself, and best of all, to reconcile the two for the happiness I'd always dreamed of, but was beginning to worry I'd never find.

Michelle

Chapter I

How Do You Know If He's The One?

If you are a woman, and you are single, you have probably asked yourself repeatedly, **"How will I know if he is the one?"** In fact, most of us ask that question every time a new guy comes into our lives, or even after we've been in a relationship for years.

It's a healthy question, but very few women know how to get the answer. That's where you need a plan, or better yet, a map. We're glad you want to take steps to move beyond the "give each guy a chance and just see where it goes" routine, which is a lot like trying to land a plane when you can't see the airstrip. Women gamble their self-esteem, emotional well-being, and years of their lives like this all the time because society doesn't offer any other way to go about it. This book will enlighten you and provide you with confidence in dating and eventually knowing if he is the "one"!

Arranged marriages are a thing of the past, and the pendulum has swung to the opposite extreme, where women regularly pick their men based on attraction and chemistry more than anything else. But the truth is, you can have your cake and eat it too, with a sensible approach to finding your mate that also happens to be fun, fun, fun!

Consider this: **there are fantastic men all around**. Yes, this is absolutely true. You've almost certainly passed some of them by because you haven't learned how to recognize them yet. I call them "diamonds in the rough" because what makes them such great partners isn't outwardly obvious to most women.

1

One of these diamonds in the rough could be your perfect match, but if I sat you down with twenty men and he was one of them, what are the chances you'd choose him? Probably slim.

> There are great men out there; perhaps it's your Picker that is broken!

I myself experienced the same dilemma, but only after I had been through a marriage with a man that wasn't compatible with me and a serious relationship with another man that was even less compatible with me! My current husband is the man of my dreams. But when I first met him, I didn't think so! Like virtually all of us, I was operating with the wrong standards to find the right guy. My radar was not working for me, so I completely passed him over! He didn't seem like the man of my dreams. He didn't look or act like the man of my dreams. He didn't have the background of the man of my dreams. And I certainly didn't feel any chemistry with him. I just didn't know how to pick the right guy for me, and I'm sure you have often faced the same dilemma. I would have missed out on this "perfect guy for me" if it wasn't for one life altering experience. It dawned on me that my skills for choosing men had a bad track record. I accepted it, and was willing to finally try something new. Something that worked. I emphasize this because I want you to know that a world of incredible possibilities will emerge when you embrace the fact that the advice we have swallowed and used as our mate matching by-laws for years, simply does NOT work!

If you feel disillusioned, distrustful or you simply wonder how you will know when you've met the right one, this plan/map will revolutionize your thinking, and in the end, you will probably be surprised with **the man who you'll discover is your perfect mate!**

Like me, you might resist him when you first meet him, but if you follow the plan, your propensity to choose based on chemistry will be righted by the fact that your love for him will bowl you over one day, and then you will know with perfect clarity that he IS the one!

Now back to my story. Luckily, while my future husband was still in the periphery of my life, I began learning how not to choose men based on face value. I'd already learned a thing or 5,000 about men, but this new wisdom really clicked.

I found out how to take my time discovering the real fiber of a man's character and to have an amazing time while I was at it! I allowed the dating process (which I call 1st Gear) to be what it should be: fun! Why? Because having fun gives a man the chance to feel comfortable being himself. In fact, this step alone helped me to uncover the diamond that my husband Emmett really was, and now I can tell you emphatically that, as husbands go, he is the greatest partner that I could ever ask for. His qualities are a perfect match for me. We are completely natural and authentic together. Over time, communication has become our greatest bond. Most importantly, I feel safer and more myself than I have with any other man. He is my best friend, and I knew within 3 months of meeting him that I could spend the rest of my life with him. He has my back and I have his. We work together even when we have disagreements. There is a level of respect, honor and trust that I longed for in every other relationship before, but never knew how to find until my new found wisdom revealed how to figure out what I needed in a partner, which led me to Emmett.

> Having fun gives a man the chance to feel comfortable being himself on a date.

Picking a guy based primarily on things like whether you have fun together, or whether you are turned on by his looks will contribute to a "broken picker", which will probably end in heartache. It's okay to want those things as well, but I have to tell you that "looks" can easily change. So if you're truly ready for fulfillment, I ask you to please dig deep throughout this process, and **find out what really matters to you**. I emphasize *you*, because this isn't about what anyone else thinks. It's not about what your mother or your father thinks is a worthwhile catch, or someone your friends will be impressed by.

This is the time for deep inner reflection of the values and qualities that make you who you are, because to find the man of your dreams, you need to find **you**.

What is a SoulMate Map©?

Think of the SoulMate Map© as a recipe for your favorite meal! It's a process of figuring out which ingredients are best for both your health and happiness, then putting it all together for an ideal model of the delicious guy that's just right for you.

Like I've mentioned, it's common for women to decide which men to date based on chemistry, a mutual interest in each other, and shared interests in general. If you think about it, it's like picking a meal only because it tastes good. People also like to select the nicest looking thing on the men-u (forgive the pun), and in that case, there is no guarantee that even the flavor will be enjoyable.

> In the SoulMate Map© process you discover which qualities really matter to you.

Preferences can get complex, such as picking your man based on ingredients like social standards, education, intelligence and income. Yet for all the typical precautions in a woman's selectivity, there is still a national failure rate of over 50%, which involves painful break-ups, financial ruin, custody battles, extensive therapy and injuries to self-esteem. And before the breakup, the worst possible scenario is when you start feeling bad about yourself or suppressed, because you are in a relationship with a man who is not in sync with you, and his values, or goals, or communication style is in conflict with yours. Let me repeat this so you really get it: When you choose a man whose values, goals and communication style are in conflict with yours, the relationship is doomed to perpetual strife. Devote yourself to creating your map, and you can bypass gambling your future and risking problems like these.

> In a great relationship, communication should be your greatest bond.

We are not crystal ball compatibility testers. The SoulMate Map© process is a series of exercises for raising your awareness and opening your eyes to discovering and knowing in advance if your new love interest is worth investing your life, your home, your children's (or future children's) happiness and your heart. It involves asking you some deep and profound questions, both simple and complex, to which you will need to decide the answers (and record them).

If you have been beating yourself up for making poor choices or even feel like you can't trust your own judgment, you can say good bye to those fears by the time you're finished with your map. If it took you years to figure out that you were with the wrong man, don't be hard on yourself! Without these tools, that time-frame is pretty standard. But *with* these tools, you can finally let go of that fear of your own poor judgment that makes you feel that you can't be trusted to pick the right guy. That only happened because you never had a map before!

So in conclusion, the SoulMate Map© is a tool for discovery that will guide you through the process of figuring out those qualities and traits that are a match for you. It will also teach you how to recognize the guy who legitimately matches what's on your map as well as the ones you should cut your losses on before you become too invested. Imagine how nice it will be to know when a guy isn't a match, so you can let him go without wasting your life wondering whether you have given him enough chances!

Now, as you march into the wide world of dating experiences, you will be armed with the knowledge you need, so that you **won't have to ask yourself, "Is he the one?" You'll know.**

Let's Get Started!

Before your lessons and exercises begin, there is some invaluable information that you will need for a strong foundation to your new approach to relationships. The following knowledge is, in fact, every bit as important as building your map, so I hope you will do your best to truly take it to heart.

What is Love?

First of all, let's tackle a crazy little thing called love, shall we? When you take the time to analyze relationships that seemed fantastic at first but then ended painfully (whether they are yours or someone else's), they usually have something in common. The couples involved probably didn't look too closely at the traits, qualities and values that truly define their partner. People often fail to evaluate these things before the relationship starts, or in some cases, they never do! All they know is that they are in love, and then they take a huge leap of faith and later find out that the person they

> Feeling love is not a guarantee that you are meant to be partners for life.

6

fell in love with is not at all compatible with them! Most of us were brought up on a steady diet of stories in which love was pure magic and often happened the moment two people's eyes met! Or they believed that simply meeting each other meant that fate had extended its mysterious touch to anoint them as perfect partners for one another! In these fairy tales, each person doesn't know the first thing about the other and yet they are still completely enchanted and smitten. Then of course, they overcome external obstacles and live happily ever after.

Is there really some mysterious force out there that has predetermined your destiny? Do you believe love happens like it did in movies like "When Harry Met Sally," "Enchanted" or "Serendipity?" Do you wonder every time you meet a man if he is the one? Did your paths cross because of some cosmic or divine plan? Or is your model less Hollywood inspired, and you think that any man should be given a chance just because he shows interest? Is your secret fantasy that you'll find love when you least expect it by rushing around a corner at the same time and running into each other as your eyes meet with mutual longing and explosive desire? It's fine to be open to magic and the whole chance meeting thing. We just recommend that you apply a little science to your plan of action too, by being conscious about what makes a man worthy of your love.

If you observe relationships today, you'll probably find that outside of some fairy tale programming, adults haven't added much to their expectations on how to find their soul mate, no matter how many hardships they've been through. The result is that people wind up thinking there is something wrong with either themselves or the opposite sex, and that's as far as their investigations go!

Let's dive right into the truth about this subject! This may or may not come as a surprise, but feeling love is not a guarantee that you are meant to be partners for life.

What!?! Admit it, how many times have you convinced yourself that your feeling of love is why you didn't give up, even though the hardships were more prevalent than the good times. In reality, everyone has a personality, and how can a warm, fuzzy or fluttery feeling tell you anything about whether both your personalities and approaches to life are a match? In fact, in some cases the "love" feeling could be nothing more than a neurological high created by chemicals like endorphin, serotonin, and dopamine. But even after you discover each other's approach to life, love and relationships, the love drug tends to keep couples hooked but miserable.

Another possible pitfall to winding up in love without considering compatibility is that once you are in love, you may discover your "love languages" or "love styles" are incompatible. For instance, your need to give and receive affection is your "love style", but your husband does not express love that way. He expresses his love by going to work and being a provider. You will probably find yourself craving physical affection and more communication than he is willing to provide. The battle may then ignite heated discussions and hurtful defenses, resulting in combative barbs like he is cold and emotionless, and you are needy and relentless. Neither is true! Your "love styles" are simply incompatible. Ultimately, without the affection and communication you need in a love relationship, you are left feeling unloved, and in all likelihood, the marriage will fail whether you stay together or not. What do I mean by this? There are more ways to end a relationship than divorce or break-up.

If you choose to stay in a relationship without love and happy interaction, that relationship will end emotionally, even if you don't break up. You may still be together, but the relationship will be hollow and loveless, leaving you clinging to the futile hope that you will somehow, someday, find happiness together. Fortunately, the SoulMate Map© is designed to unearth the compatible qualities you will need for a successful love based not only on excitement and joy, but also on a deep and profound sense of mutual devotion and respect. If you are clinging to a marriage that feels hopeless, you can rely on this map to help reveal your compatibility in that relationship, to show you if you should move on, or to see if there's still a chance you could work it out.

Don't waste years of your life clinging to a hollow marriage. The best way to insulate yourself from the challenges of divorce or choosing to stay in a loveless marriage is by knowing who he really is before you get too deep into the relationship.

Women Should Hold the Relationship Reins!

Here's the first bit of crucial advice you need to embrace on your SoulMate Map© journey: **Women start, steer and end relationships**. When you really absorb this knowledge, you should feel very liberated, and better yet, it will have a profound effect on your success in relationships.

It's not true that all relationships are started and steered by women, just the ones that last, with everyone is happy! Neither does it mean that women are the boss. Nor does it mean that women are entitled to be divas at the expense of her man's happiness and self-esteem.

SoulMate Map© is all about how to "start" your relationships successfully.

Interlaced within the following lessons and exercises are nuggets of wisdom on recognizing how the importance of your happiness will help to make your relationship a success, and will make your man happy too. We're going to guide you to start trusting your gut again, instead of suppressing yourself in fear of coming off as being "difficult"! Women have an internal compass that allows them to guide relationships better than a man, generally speaking. It's just part of our make-up. This knowledge should be liberating too, and should help you make better choices based on a new found confidence in yourself.

So take the reins, because when you study the works of academic experts in **linguistics and anthropology, they will reveal that men are**, in fact, not wired to recognize the details and nuances of a relationship like women are. Men come in all shapes, sizes and temperaments, with their own kinds of strength and wisdom! But according to the experts, women were built to steer relationships! While men's judgment in relationships can be pretty good if they are awake and really devoted to studying what works, yours will almost always be better. Here is the secret: use those reins from an approach of partnership. Demonstrate to him that not only are you going to communicate clearly and responsibly, but you also have his back. Show him that you will lead the partnership as a partner and not as what men fear: a woman who is all about herself, hard to please, and bent on taking away all his freedom. **When you learn the skills you need to guide and lead, fostering cooperation without allowing yourself to become suppressed, then you will have a very happy man**. Both of you will feel fabulous love and freedom! Your guy will be deeply satisfied and willing to do whatever you enjoy doing, because he knows you understand and fulfill his needs too. Ultimately, it's a pure and trusting sense that together, you can soar like you never could apart!

> Do you take for granted that Men's and Women's brains are wired differently?

Why is a woman's brain usually wired better to guide relationships than a man's? Well, have you noticed that you tend to analyze, notice, care, wonder, worry, and communicate to a degree that men typically can't match? It is a well-documented biological fact that women have adapted to handle a higher level of social complexity than men. When a woman's brain is inspected under brain imaging and compared to a man's, scientists have found that there are more connections across the corpus callosum, which controls the ability to engage both hemispheres of the brain. The corresponding parts of a woman's brain light up more during typical activities related to emotions and areas used for relationship management. Therefore you, goddess, hold the key to successful relationships!

So, should you choose a man simply because he chooses you? Sounds like a silly question, but **unfortunately, many relationships are started this way, and will have a high failure rate**. Why would so many women blindly go along with this? Often, one's self-esteem hungering for male desire and attention is the driving force behind this blunder. Because these women lack confidence and the awareness of what they have to offer, instead they are blinded by the need to feel loved. To compound things, women in this situation generally haven't developed a very strong idea of who they want as a partner. They just want to be wanted.

Why the high failure rate with this type of situation? The problem is the result of "trying to make it work" with any guy who shows interest in you. Just because he shows interest in you is not a valid reason for trying on a relationship with him. I recognize this approach from my own life. I remember thinking, "Has he been put into my life for a reason?" Or the scary reality is that I was so flattered that some took interest in me, that I didn't consider my own feelings, because my radar for love hadn't been so great. Yes, I had a broken picker. But the truth is, you are giving your power away when you do that. Quite frankly, we entertain giving guys who show interest in us a chance because we lack clarity about what we deserve in a partner. As a result, you are entering the relationship blindfolded, because you don't look at whether he truly has the characteristics of a good partner for YOU! If you don't know what will make you happy in the areas of partnership and companionship, you will spend your life simply stumbling over failed relationship after failed relationship. Relationships that only make you unhappy. Sorting out what you don't want after you are already trapped in a bad relationship is painful! So I plan to help you figure out what you want now!

Your first step is to honor the fact that **you have a powerful role in determining how a relationship is started, steered, and possibly ended.** Honoring this can help guide both of you to success.

The Entitled Man!

> Without even realizing it, you placed his happiness as the focus of the relationship.

If a relationship generally follows what a man wants and decides, the woman will usually feel either neglected or suppressed. You've met that guy, haven't you? He goes off and does what he wants, and leaves the woman alone and lonely. Or he has affairs, because he does not see what he risks losing, and you set the tone for it all by accepting his crumbs and anointing him the "object" of the relationship's happiness! From day one, you started the relationship by proving to him that you know what it takes to make him happy. Without even realizing it, you placed his happiness as the focus of the relationship, and in that same moment, you unwittingly sealed your destiny as the neglected second citizen, while killing off the chance for true partnership. There is just the king and you, the devotee who takes care of herself.

Let me tell you a true story. I am guilty of this very same "start" to a relationship. In my early twenties, I met my future first husband. Like most women at that age, I was an open book and ready to experience new things. Where having fun was concerned, I didn't really know what I liked or didn't like yet. So in the courting stage (I call it 2nd gear in the dating cycle) of our relationship, if he came up with something new to do that I had never done before, I would go because I did not know yet whether I would enjoy that activity or not. For instance, one time he took me river-tubing. "Wow, that sounds fun!" Every week of 2nd gear, he kept coming up with new fun things to do that I simply could not say no to. My date/future hubby (let's call him Romeo, since he was actively courting me) was fun, playful, spontaneous and adventurous - all things I like in a man. He was attentive, he adored me, and he was majorly in love with me. He had a great disposition and we enjoyed our conversations. Check, check, check! Now here is where the relationship took the wrong turn. I didn't know what I wanted in the long-term, so I was just discovering my preferences underlinepassively as the relationship progressed.

I did what most women do; **I let my man choose for me**. He fell in love with my willingness to do anything, which he called my sense of adventure. And rather than ruin his love for me, I kept being that person. But it turns out; I am not very adventurous after all. I don't like thrill seeking, adrenaline provoking activities. And not only that, after I tried something once or twice, if I did not like it, I didn't want to try to improve my skills until I did like it! It turned out that my husband was an adventure junkie who loved competition and being the center of attention. Neither of those traits were good husband material for me. But things didn't end then, believe it or not. Why? Because I, like so many other women, chose to ignore that intuition! Instead I continued to engage myself in **whatever he wanted to make him happy**. This is the key point. We NEVER did anything I wanted; unless it happened to be something he wanted to do. So you can see, I started the relationship by setting a standard of self-suppression, unaware of what I needed to be happy in the long term, and pretending to be what he wanted.

So when the relationship hit 3rd gear, the phase when you really need to discuss what you want in a partnership and be clear about your needs, you guessed it, I wimped out! I said nothing and just allowed him to declare the future of **my** life. In 1st gear, the dating stage, I clearly was in charge. But when we got somewhere in the middle of 2nd gear, I acquiesced and became one of those women who does everything to please her man, all the while forgetting herself. A healthy relationship/partnership includes both people's needs. Your happiness is just as important as his.

Any relationship where the woman's happiness is not actively pursued will be a dead and unfulfilling relationship for both parties. Never underestimate the power of a woman's happiness and what it provides for men. Our happiness is their catnip. It's what causes men to do great things, to be inspired, and to grow and be better men. Any man that is deliciously happy in a relationship is that way not only because you care about his happiness, but because he gets a lot of **gratification** from the rewards of **your** happiness. So later, when you make your SoulMate Map©, be sure to include that **you want a man that is devoted to your happiness**. One of my secret weapons to great relationships – Guaranteed!

The ultimate lesson in my story is that I did not start the relationship based on what I wanted. I did not even give any real thought to it. The SoulMate Map© was designed to prevent situations like these. If I'd had it then, not only would it have provided me with some personal power, I would also have known that I wanted a man that enjoyed the arts, that was ambitious, and shared my approach to spending, budgeting and planning for our future. Romeo never liked to discuss anything that pertained to feelings, which was my "love style", so trying to connect with him emotionally was torture and left me

> Women start, steer and end relationships.

feeling very alone. Also, I never expressed my firm stand on fidelity, because like most women, I just assumed he knew that cheating on me would break my heart. It may seem like an obvious no-no to you, but don't blindly assume that a man will know that. Romeo had many opportunities to play with other women because I didn't inform him of my standards in fidelity and I gave him free rein to do things without me. Both these factors opened the door to opportunities for infidelity without fear of consequences, for him.

Another one of my great lessons from that relationship, which went into my SoulMate Map©, is that I needed a man who not only loved me for my generosity, but participated with me in acts of generosity. Romeo was annoyed with my generosity. He did everything in his power to suppress it, and I allowed it, until one day, my spirit was gone and I died inside and was chronically unhappy. So then the marriage died. I am now married to a husband that matches me in the generosity department. He is the most compatible partner I could ever ask for. With him, I made it very clear how important fidelity is, and how I need a man that would never hurt me that way. He has respected that need beautifully. If you haven't guessed, he scores very high on my SoulMate Map©!

A Word on Steering Relationships

This is another absolutely crucial lesson, so please do your best to embrace it. If I had been clearer with Romeo about what I wanted, spoke up more and made more requests, then perhaps things would have changed in our marriage. Any relationship that has a strong foundation for love and compatibility can flourish again if the woman is willing to take the reins and begin steering the partnership. Communication is the key to success in this steering process. If a man revels in your happiness, how can he be successful if you don't help him discover the things that make you happy? When a man wants to make his woman happy, and she takes the reins and shows him - that is a relationship model that always wins!

This is such a big concept, that is so profound, so important, you can't even imagine. And this is the art of steering. There is much to learn and master, but that's as far as we will delve into that subject here. Of course I want you to master how to steer a relationship, therefore I encourage you to join our email lists so you can learn of upcoming programs.

Some of Your Best Information Comes From Failure!

My ex-husband Romeo was and is a sweet and lovely man. He has great qualities and there is nothing wrong with his approach to marriage or relationships, except that he was not a match for me! I learned so much about myself in my experiences with him, it would have been quite a shame if I let that knowledge go to waste.

I once was in love with a man who was a single dad and lived in the same town for his entire 30-something years. When I opened a discussion on how he felt about travel, he said he never had. The only travel he had ever ventured on was to an amusement park in the next state. Of course there were many other reasons why I could see our lives were not a match, including his parenting style, but the point is, the travel was much too important to me, and it really was a clear sign of the major differences we had that would eventually drive a huge wedge between us.

On the opposite side of the spectrum, I discovered during the 2nd Gear courting stage of my relationship with my current husband, (It's important that you remember he is my idea of a dream husband!) that he had traveled, but never beyond the contiguous 48 states. He didn't even have a passport? What? Not even a passport! So naturally, this was a conversation we had to have before going forward.

Rather than making assumptions, I plowed in further to find out why his travel experience was so limited. My biggest mistake would have been to jump to conclusions, based on the last guy who did not like to travel.   It turns out that he was married to a woman who did not fly, and therefore he did not have much experience with it. He himself had no issue with traveling abroad. It was his ex-wife's preference/fear of flying that was the culprit. Since we have been married, he has been thrilled to discover the experience of new cultures and landscapes, so it turns out that we are a match in the travel department after all, even though it didn't seem that way at first! I can't say our match on that quality is perfect. I have to push sometimes, but he is flexible, which is what I need in a partner. Rigid and stubborn does not work for me, which you can be sure I added to my list #1 (red flag list) as a result of being in love with "Mr. Charming but Stubborn Romeo", who I told you about at the start of this journey.

So, when you look back on your failed relationships, if you understand and take ownership of the role you played, like maybe you acquiesced and did not start or steer your man or the relationship, then perhaps you can free yourself of any anger or resentment you may be harboring.

Men can be **oblivious to what women want, need and are hinting at**. A great woman doesn't torture her man for his lack of woman savvy. Instead, she helps him by using the steering principles, and acknowledges that she has to be a better soul mate picker. You'll be given exercises to help you use the lessons of each past relationship experience, and gather that priceless information to help you develop a great SoulMate Map©.

The Best Mate For You?

The SoulMate Map© is designed to uncover your best match by guiding you through a deep self-analysis. Therefore, its success depends enormously on one key ingredient: authenticity. If you truly want to save yourself endless heartache and time lost on trial and error, you will need to be honest with yourself. The exercises will help you with that. You're not just going to find out about the kind of partner you need, you're going to find out what kind of partner **you** are. Never give answers based on who you want to be, rather than the real you. For instance, saying you want someone who is active (because it's a good thing to wish for) and yet you never find time to be active yourself, would be a mismatch, a lie. Pretending to be interested in sports just to attract a guy won't work. You can always try it out and see if you like it, but if you find you don't, you shouldn't hide that. Saying you value generosity when the secret truth is that you know deep down inside you tend towards being selfish or self-focused could create a marriage made in hell.

Don't be afraid to be totally honest! It's not like you are being asked to reveal your secrets to anyone. No one is requesting that you stand on a stage and declare, "Hi, my name is Amy, I am a non-recovering self-absorbed partner." Hey, if that is the way you roll, then I suggest you find a mate that adores you for that, too. You want someone who loves your strengths and flaws! I hope that makes sense to you. Performances can't last forever, and when they end, they will create a rift between you and your man, leaving him with an impression like, "What happened to the fun girl I fell in love with? She used to love sports!" The better match for you would be a guy who would be happy with you whether you liked sports or not. So, as you fill out the upcoming exercises, be as honest with yourself as you can. You will create a better map.

I hope you are starting to see the light! Why wait and find you are incompatible later just because you did not give the process adequate forethought?

Confidence

For now, the last thing I want to mention is the confidence this process will bring to you! If you are feeling burned out or like you don't trust yourself to choose well, raise your hand! Here is the good news. You are on the verge of a huge change because now you know that your past criteria for choosing men didn't work! You may have had a broken picker! But it's not your fault. You were just doing what every other person is doing and that is why we have a 50%-60% divorce rate. If the divorce rate is that high, can you just imagine who how high the dating failure rate is? If you dated five people before meeting the "one" you felt like marrying, then five out of six relationships did not last. That's over 80% that failed.

Don't get me wrong. I believe we all can grow from our serial relationships, but the point I am making is, "What would life be like if you had more clarity about the right person for you?" Wouldn't it be great if you passed on a guy earlier on, because you looked at your SoulMate Map© and recognized that there were some show stopping reasons why your partnership wouldn't last? Imagine feeling free and confident because you now know how to spot a man that is really into you **and** is compatible with you! Now that vision can become a reality.

Chapter 2

Give Yourself Time to Learn!

Step 1: Take a Break

The first thing you have to do if you are not already in a relationship is: Stop dating! Right now! Make up your mind to take a breather, or at the very least, instead of dating to find a mate, only date for fun and social interaction. You are officially off the market for a relationship! Remove the intention to find "the man of your dreams" or even "a boyfriend". Think of men as someone to have a good time with and nothing else. Don't worry about how compatible they are, or if they want the same things you do. It doesn't matter, they are just dates, and you need to declare that you are not looking for a partner right now.

> "Just date for fun, until your SoulMate Map is complete"

What do you do once you've decided to take a break? Do some work! The most successful way to improve your love life would be to start by looking at your patterns! Some patterns are effective, but some are not. In fact, you may not even recognize that you have patterns. The truth is, they are there. Everyone has them. Maybe unbeknownst to you, you have patterns about how you date, how you perceive certain male types, how you start relationships, how you communicate with men and so forth.

As a relationship coach, after I work with clients and help them to identify where their soul mate picker is broken and help them choose new patterns, they are blown away by the quality of men that come into their life. It's as though something changed in them, so now the jerks just aren't appealing and there is a well-spring of mutual attraction with great guys!

Step 1 Assignment

Write down a declaration that you will take a break, and explain how that will look. Start with a statement that will empower you! Something like: "I am officially off the market. Now I will just date for fun and I don't even care if a guy is "my type" anymore.

Write your declaration now:

Step 2: Get Busy!

Taking a break from looking for a great partner can be hard if you don't know what to do with yourself in the meantime, so we want you to have access to this second lesson right away! It's important to change your daily activities to support your new, deliberately single life.

Boredom is usually the first enemy. It can lead to poor choices, like poking around dating sites out of curiosity and sending back intimate emails and texts to men you casually meet there. (And by the way, you'll burn bridges by establishing intimacy in emails, texts and phone calls before you even meet in person!) It's very important to find fulfilling things to do with your time.

Instead of locking yourself up at home, **get busy having fun with your life!** Fill your time doing things you enjoy! Spend time with friends. Use this period of breathing space to do things for yourself that you haven't yet gotten around to doing. Perhaps it's a good time to discover the joy of doing things alone! What's so great about that? Everything! Be open to learning a lesson about yourself, by at least giving it a try. You might find you are the type of person that can enjoy going out to a movie by yourself, or grabbing a bite to eat, perhaps with just some reading material for company. Be confident doing things by yourself (if you aren't already)! You're not going solo because you don't have a choice; you're going solo because you do have a choice! You are fun, free and fabulous! In fact, you'll have to stick to your resolve, because nothing draws men more than a woman who is having fun, because that's when women are most approachable. Besides, when you are alone having a good time, a healthy man wouldn't think, "Gee, what is wrong with her? She is alone. Instead he would think, "Wow, I've got to go over there and meet her! She looks fun!" Normally a guy has to devise clever schemes of penetrating a frustrating roadblock of friends if he wants to meet you, so stick to your guns, because whatever enjoyment you'll get burying yourself in your computer searching for men is ultimately part of a broken pattern!

Another powerful reason for being busy is that doing things that are fun, will give off a great vibe that you love your life. Men are more attracted to women who radiate fun while enjoying life than women who are bored and lonely. You won't have to prove to anyone that you are a "fun" person. You'll be radiating it! Think about it for a moment. Would you really want to attract a man who is turned on by women who are lonely and bored? Seriously, can you imagine some guy thinking, "Oh, look at her. She is lonely. Let me ask her out and brighten her life!" Heck no! What kind of healthy male would find this to be a great opportunity? The only guys who you will be attracting will be control freaks or men who prey on vulnerable women. So get busy filling your life with fun and discovering what makes you happy!

Because this step will help you solidify your confidence, you should find it easier to be boldly honest when you create your SoulMate Map©. Not only that, but it will also further develop the quiet power that will help you embrace your role as the "steerer" of a successful relationship.

What Will You Do?

Now let's get more specific about ways you can spend your time. What projects have you been meaning to start or finish? What classes or lessons have you always said you wanted to take? What books would you like to get lost in?

If you still want the company of the opposite sex, maybe it's time to take dance lessons. Salsa is a spicy exhilarating choice where it's not assumed that you want to do anything more than just dance. Or you could join a guitar class, or maybe a book group. Choose an activity that you love and then find a group of people who share the same level of interest in that activity.

Warning: Don't follow your old patterns of scoping out which men are attractive. You are NOT looking for a love interest. Remember, you gave up the pattern of keeping your eyes peeled for interesting men wherever you go! This step is all about you finding what's fun and thinking of men only as people you could have fun with, not potential dates or mates. Even if you are asked out on a date, maintain the Zen of just having fun, and not wondering if he is someone worth dating.

For extra support, enroll your friends or family in helping you stay strong. Let them know you are taking a break from dating and need their support in staying busy.

Step 2 Assignment

What will you do differently to keep busy?

Are you willing to stop using dating sites or going wherever you normally go to look for men, and instead go out and do things you enjoy doing instead? What activities will you stop in order to curb the impulse? What new activities will you take on? Who will you enroll in your new plan, so you have friends around to have fun with and to help you relieve the need to look for Mr. Not Right Now!

List of changes you will make

Write your list now. Be sure to include activities that not only empower you, but also help you discover and develop your awareness of what makes you happy!

Chapter 3

Discover Your Happiness

Step 3: Find Your Happiness

Now that you are beginning to explore activities that you enjoy, let's kick it up a notch and identify the things that make you happy! I hear *The Sound of Music* calling: "Raindrops on roses and whiskers on kittens... these are a few of my favorite things!" Well if that sounds silly, let me give you the real incentive.

Think about the old saying, "Happy Wife, Happy Life!" That saying was created by men. Ignoring it is hazardous to your relationship health! This is perhaps one of the most powerful insights about men, and the core of what they want in a relationship. **More than any one thing, or any one trait, or quality, or appearance, when a man is in love, he wants to know his woman is HAPPY**! Important note: "In love" was the operative phrase. Clue: If he does not seem to care about your happiness, he is not in love! Repeat: Any man that is not focused on actively pursuing your happiness is not in love! And wanting to spend time with you does not equal being devoted to your happiness. There is a subtle but completely different behavior involved with those two motivations.

> "Men in love, focus on your happiness!"

> "Red flag: He was uncaring about what makes me happy"

Think about it. Haven't you heard a former boyfriend or husband say, "All I want is for you to be happy?" Why? Because when you are happy you are a joy to be with. A happy woman is heaven on earth for men. Not only are you a delight to be with, but it also means that you are not challenging him with your unhappiness. And why is your unhappiness a challenge? Because, dear student, men are confused about what to do when you are unhappy. Your unhappiness is trouble with a capital **T**.

Before you begin to master the important nuances of understanding how men deal with a woman's unhappiness, let's just start you on a new direction towards sourcing your own happiness.

First of all, faking being happy is ineffectual. You can't just sit there and say, "Okay, if what men want is a happy woman, I will simply show happiness." That is NOT my coaching. The last thing I want you to be is a person who suppresses her feelings, or pretends. The lesson about being truly happy while expressing your needs is a BIG lesson.

Right now, while you are taking your "break" from dating, use this time to develop a new skill and awareness by exploring your happiness. If you glaze over this step, then forget about the SoulMate Map©. The map won't work if you don't comprehend the power in your happiness. You may pick a better guy, but you won't have that off-the-charts happy, yummy love! Furthermore, knowing what you enjoy and what makes you happy are key elements in developing your SoulMate Map© in the first place. That is why you are asked to do it now, instead of later. It's all part of the secret recipe!

Step 3 Assignment

Discover what makes you happy!

Spend your next few months paying attention to what makes you happy. (Not the worst assignment, right?) That also includes taking the time to do the things that make you happy. Do you like to ride a bike through beautiful parks? Do you like to get massages? Do you like to spend time with girlfriends? Take hot baths? Cook fantastic food? Tend a garden? Explore museums? Change your focus inward and use this time to know yourself and what makes you happy. Because when you get to step six, you will to need know this. Take time to continuously add to your happiness list, because it will evolve over time. Here is how you should record it:

Start a journal and label a few pages at the top with "My happiness discoveries:" or "I really enjoy:" or "I notice I am happy when:" *or come up with a different title that inspires you!*

Keep coming back to it!

What's Next?

In the next section, we are going to teach you some new standards that will prep you for designing the best possible SoulMate Map© for your unique personality. If you were to just design one today, you might not have the inspiration or awareness of what "must haves" you should include for the man that will come into your life. These standards are not only what every woman should want for themselves, but without them, you'll risk wasting time on men who are not relationship material.

After embracing these new standards, you'll start discovering how to tell whether a man is truly into you in a way that will sustain through time, kids, life challenges and aging, or fooling you into thinking he loves you. Then, you'll start designing your SoulMate Map©. It's a process designed to help you discover who is your perfect mate is in a way that you almost certainly have never explored to this depth before.

Chapter 4

Perhaps Your Standards Are Too Low

Step 4: Raise Your Bar

"Why do women waste their time on the unworthy men?"

What comes to your mind when I say, "Raise Your Bar?" I know many of you will probably think the obvious: "Raise your standards in your choice of men." That, of course, is followed by the typical reply: "I've been accused of being too picky!" This is where we need to get specific.

If you've been told you are too picky, that's because first off, along with your high standards, there is probably some tendency to be unrealistic about what qualities to focus on. Secondly, you may have been hurt in the past so you became picky as a way to avoid repeating your past mistakes.

However, raising your standards in your choice of men is only a part of the challenge. There are three more pieces to the puzzle. 1. You must also raise your awareness of the power you have over men. 2. You must know the importance of your role as the guiding force in a relationship. 3. You must accept the true value of yourself, your happiness and your personal standards. **Raising your bar is the holy grail** of messages I want every woman to hear and understand! I think only 10% of the population has a healthy "bar" level. I want you to drop old broken dating and mate selection patterns that were developed by the "unclued" masses. Popular relationship models are dysfunctional, and you need to wean yourself off that kind of programming. Better yet, quit cold-turkey! How about some standards to challenge your thinking? Read on!

Choosing Based on Appearances

If your criteria for choosing a guy is primarily based on his looks, I want you to take a breath, and look deeper into his heart. Observe the qualities of his personality, his ethics, his values, his approach to family, his approach to caring, and his humanity.

How about breaking the habit by implementing a completely basic but still incredibly wise philosophy that has already been ingrained in you? That philosophy is, "Don't judge a book by its cover!" The next time you find yourself zeroing in on men with an attractive appearance, repeat that phrase in your mind.

Accepting Crumbs

How many times have you accepted, and made excuses for, a man who was selfish and did things that clearly showed you that he didn't care about your feelings, happiness or well-being? You know there is a book that touches on this topic, called, "He's just not that into you." You can't change him, but you can stop settling and making excuses. Now don't go all Rambo on him and become a woman who trashes men who do thoughtless things! Instead, **just move on**. The fact is, it's not your place to educate a man who you've just started dating. Besides, he has no vested interest in caring what you think, and may just dismiss you as being neurotic.

The most important question here is, "Why are *you* settling?" For example, if a guy lied to you, why would

"No one is going to respect you if you don't respect yourself!"

you ever go out with him again? Do you want to be involved with a liar? Take a stand and walk away! No drama, just be clear you deserve better and walk away.

A tale from a woman accepting crumbs

Her last relationship left her depleted , a mere shell of her former self. Her pattern was to give all of herself to her partner while diminishing herself to keep him from being upset. She now sees that she did this to herself. But she also sees that she chose partners that were not devoted to her happiness and she had been accepting crumbs. Her idea of how to be a partner was to give and give, ignoring the fact that her efforts were one sided.

She came to me and said the greatest gift she had gotten from this process is that she found her self worth again. The list making was a healing process resulting in reclaiming awareness for herself and her happiness. She won't ever give that power away again.

Stop Accepting the Lies

The example of men lying is worth discussing further, as it is a frequent trait in the kinds of guys that will be below your standards from now on!

> "Lying and cheating are <u>now</u> below your standards!"

I've dealt with this issue extensively, myself. In fact, men lied to me all the time throughout my life. That behavior often goes hand in hand with cheating, which I also dealt with extensively! It was a common pattern for me, and it might be a common pattern for you. But cheating and lying aren't common patterns for me anymore. Care to know why? Well, it all stopped the day that I stopped accepting that level of disrespect. It all depends on you taking a stand for yourself. Accept the fact that you deserve better, because you do. I'm going to share an interesting story with you on this subject.

I remember one situation when I was dating this guy, and I told him that I would only have sex with someone who was exclusive. He told me he understood and would respect my wishes. But you know, I could feel it in my gut that he was not sincere. In fact, I could tell something was off just by the way he talked to me. He was fabulously wealthy and had just gotten out of a marriage that ended badly. He knew how to act like a man in a relationship, but there were signs that he was being secretive, and he knew how to set things up so he could hide the truth.

He invited me to go on an extended weekend vacation in the Caribbean, all on him. Two nights before we were supposed to leave, I came over to his house without giving him much notice. It wasn't intentional. It just happened that way. In fact, he wanted me to have dinner and spend the night. So far, so good. Then, at some point while I was there that evening, I saw two wine glasses in the sink, one with lipstick. I questioned him about it and he had some vague excuse. That feeling in my gut that something was wrong rang out clearer than ever.

You may have had that sensation yourself. It should not be confused with fear or jealousy. It's just one of those female instincts.

Later that night, we were in bed talking, and he slipped and said something that did not fit in with his other stories. So while he was asleep I got up, feeling restless about my foreboding instincts. When I passed his desk, I spotted a card. Normally I wouldn't peek, but like the wine glasses, it wasn't hidden, and at that point, I was sure he wasn't telling me the truth. Sure enough, it was a love note from another woman. So, uncharacteristically, I left in the middle of the night. There was no grand argument or emotional explosion. I just left.

The next day, he called to ask what happened. I told him. He started crafting more lies, but I stood my ground. Then he finally admitted the truth, and I made a decision that was hard for me. I decided not to go with

"Respect for myself was more important than any free vacation"

him on the vacation. The former "low bar" me would have gone anyway, justifying that it's cruel to leave him last minute, since he spent all that money, or I might have gone anyway just to treat myself to a vacation. But what it really boiled down to was respect for myself, which is more important than any free vacation.

You know what? That experience marked the beginning where I took my first real stand. That was when I started honoring my self-worth even though it meant walking away from great temptation. Do you think he would have cared if I was upset but chose to go anyway? Or if I refused to go but didn't break things off? No, he would have assumed that, like most women, I would give him whatever he wanted with enough time and enough bribes. And if I went anyway and tortured him by being cold to him, how much fun or satisfaction would that have been? Really, it would only make me look bad, and would have nothing to do with teaching him a lesson. The moral of the story, which you absolutely need to learn, is that no one is going to respect you if you don't respect yourself!

Respecting Yourself

Let's talk more about the value of you! Take a moment to think about ways in which you demonstrate that you don't respect yourself? When you've started seeing a guy and he breaks a date once, you can give him the benefit of the doubt. But if he does it twice, let him go! If he is a decent guy, he will feel bad and make it up to you. If he really is thoughtless, and does not try to make amends, then he is not worth your time. Letting him go does not mean you should berate him for not respecting you.

> Just be clear you deserve better and be willing to walk away

Walking away doesn't even mean that you dump him. Walking away is my version of taking a break. By not being attached and being willing to be silent and nonresponsive not only gives you time to avoid over reacting, but it also sends him a message. What's the message? He does not know yet. By saying nothing, you are leaving him wondering. "Is she upset with me?" "Did I lose her?" "Is she dating someone else?" If he is truly interested, he will find out. Give him a few days before you respond.

This is not a game. Actually, it could be an opportunity that reveals his true nature and intentions. A player won't bother contacting you. It's possible an insecure or shy man won't contact you either, though I doubt a shy or insecure man would gamble losing you by engaging in sexual activity with more than one woman. The point is this... If a man has good intentions, and really is into you, discovering the consequences of his actions will bother him and he will do his best to repair things with you. But if you confront him, he won't be present to the consequences as effectively. Instead, he will be dealing with your upset and may be so distracted by figuring out how to calm you down, that he might miss the significance of his actions. So the time you give him to think and wonder during your silence is good contemplative time. It's up to you to give him that time to ponder.

It's possible that he does have a life that is complicated and it was not carelessness that caused him to break plans more than once. However, if he doesn't have time for you now, when things are usually at their most exciting, what can you expect in the future? The overarching point is that if you raise your bar and set a standard that you won't get involved with a guy who does not make the effort to win you over, you won't be emotionally invested enough to even want to rake him over the coals. That would be a useless waste of energy, anyway.

Out of the self-respect that you deserve, you must decide to say, "He is a nice guy, but I am only interested in a man who has time for me, and who thinks I'm the greatest woman he has ever met!" Notice there isn't any anger or malice in this new standard. No need to teach him a lesson. Instead, wish him well and simply categorize him in your head as a nice person who just isn't right for you, or it's not the right time. Notice there is no drama, no hurt feelings, no male bashing. Just clean respectful conversation. Don't assume he's a bad person; instead, assume he has different priorities and values, so he is not your match.

"The only guy you will consider as a potential committed partner is someone who demonstrates that he is devoted to your happiness."

Devoted to Your Happiness

Now let's take the discussion of what you deserve one step further. This step in raising your bar will probably change your life the most. Here it is: Be clear that the only guy you will consider as a committed partner is someone who demonstrates that he is **devoted to your happiness**. What does this look like? He asks you what you want to do! He takes pleasure in seeing your happiness! He loves spending time with you! This devotion to your happiness is especially obvious in the early stages when he is falling for you and wooing you. His attention is actually focused on learning about what, how, when, and where you are happy. If you don't squelch it by saying things like, "Oh, I don't care, let's do what you want," then you will actually see this remarkable devotion in action.

So, when you are with a guy who cares more about his own pleasure and activities, and he never inquires about what you want or like, move on. This is especially crucial if you are feeling attached to him. His lack of interest in what you like and enjoy is a red flag that he is not in love. If you're not convinced you should move on, maybe you just need to downgrade your exclusivity and be open to someone new.

One really good test of a man's intentions is to find out if his heart is true. Don't rely on his words. Instead, pay attention to his actions. He can say he loves you, and he can even say he can't live without you, but if his actions just don't reflect that, then you know it's not healthy love. He can think he loves you in his mind, but a sure clue that this man will bring you heartache will be revealed to you by his actions. A man with a healthy relationship outlook who is truly in love will pay close attention to what you like, he will go out of his way, he will make room for you, and he will stretch his comfort zone. He'll do whatever it takes to prove to you that he loves you.

This means only YOU have the power to short change yourself. If you want to accept crumbs from a man by placing more faith in his words than his actions, then you are blowing it! You must realize there are all types of love. There is possessive love; there is abusive love, neglectful love, indulgent love, lazy love, getting laid love, and so on. But if your goal is to achieve the kind of love imbued with mutual support and caring, the kind that is filled with respect and fun, where you know you will grow together as time endures, then please upgrade your new standards for love and say "pass" to any man who can speak love beautifully, but treats you badly, or takes you for granted. That is a love you don't want.

Here is something else to watch out for: If you are with a guy who lavishes you with attention, gifts and great dates, pay attention to whether he provides what HE thinks you would want, rather than the things that you've clearly expressed that you want. Of course, to do that, you will have had to have been expressing what you want.

A friend of mine was courted by her boyfriend with poems, flowers and romantic dinners. But the warning sign that she ignored was that he never wanted to do anything she wanted to do. Translation: he was not pursuing her happiness! He was imposing his idea of

38

what should make her happy. Did she like the flowers? Yes, generally. But he often sent her flowers she did not like. But this was the big red flag that she ignored: She would often suggest a concert or a local band she wanted to hear. He would refuse, and instead immediately divert her attention to something else. One instance of his not going, might not be a red flag, but watching bands was a passion of hers, and yet he would never go. Sure enough, in their marriage, not only would he not go to concerts with her, but he would give her such a hard time if she then wanted to go with friends, that she had to give up something she loved. **A man in love wants to get it right**. Especially in the beginning, he will go to that concert or movie that you want to go to, even if it's not to his taste. A man who wants to control you with his love won't care what you want or what makes you happy. He is out to fulfill his personal mental image about what the relationship should be like.

Another true story: A man I was once engaged to told me he was going to surprise me with the greatest weekend of my life. It was more than a vacation, it was a once in a lifetime event! I was excited, based on how he would tantalize me with the bits of clues he would tell me. He built it up by telling me things like, "You will be blown away by the glamour and excitement!" He even said that all I would have to do was just pack a variety of clothing, including a bathing suit and evening wear. I should bring my best clothes. He wouldn't even tell me the location, because that would ruin the surprise. This was going to be a weekend that I would remember always. Fast forward, and the weekend never happened. He could not work it all out. Believe it or not, this was not the disappointing part! The event that he was going to take me to was a ring side seat at the title boxing event of the world's heavy-weight fights in Las Vegas.

That might impress some of you. And even as I tell it, I have to admit that getting seats to that would have been a coup! But for me, it proved that he was clueless about what I think is special and what would make me happy. The idea of sitting ring side while men batter each other's faces and splatter me with sweat and blood is not my idea of glamorous! Thank goodness his plans failed, because I would have been horrified. So as you can see, it was all about what he wanted, and what he thought "should" make me happy regardless of what really would. If I knew then what I know now about men and the significance of a man's actions towards achieving my happiness, I would have had all the clues right then that this relationship would end badly. And it did! So approach these assignment as if you are uncovering the secrets that will help you know with certainty whether you are with a keeper or a man whose love isn't right for you.

Don't Make Men Guess

Now here is an important caveat! Men are not good at guessing what you want. So if you are of the belief that he should notice what you like and what you are interested in, then you don't understand men. Just because he does not notice does not mean he does not care. He's a man, and remember, there is a huge body of scientific research supporting that there are big differences between a male and a female brain. Men typically don't observe women's signals, signals that are obvious to other women..They also are likely to interpret these signals in a completely different way than women do. Of course, some men are the exception, but this seems to be the general rule.

One observation I have noticed about men in relationships is they want to "get it right", but when they are expected to interpret your statements, they have a 50/50 chance of getting it wrong. So many times I have overheard men muttering to themselves after their woman

40

has walked away… "Oh, that is just a set up for me to fail", or the most common statement is "I can't win!" Those three little words have big meaning for a man. **Men just want to win.** They want to win at being a man that you are happy with. They want to win at providing for you. They want to win at being a man! And what women have not realized is that in this age of woman's liberation and equality, decent men, the kind of men that are respectful to women are confused by our messages. They are left wondering how to be a strong man you respect, while honoring your need to be heard and be independent.

The way to balance this new equality partnership is to understand that a man who wants you to be happy is looking for clear communication from you.

Saying things like, "go to the store and pick up some bread" is not clear communication. Have you seen the bread isle lately? OMG, there are so many selections, you could spend 30 minutes reading all those labels.

"Provide men with the information they need to know about what makes you happy!"

Therefore, saying something specific like: "Will you pick up Orville's multi-grain bread for me? It has a yellow label, which might help you to find it faster." On the flip side, what if you didn't give him the specifics and he came home with Wonder bread. You know, white bread. Do you think you will be happy with him? No! So basically, by not being specific, you just set him up to NOT win. I cannot impress upon you more, just how HUGE, this concept is.

Other examples on how to give men good information:

When he asks you what you feel like eating in preparation to going out to dinner. Don't say "anything". Give him some choices. "Hmm, I feel in the mood for either Italian or hamburgers tonight. But if you have been craving a steak all day, it's completely fine to say, "I've had steak on my brain all day today. Would you be up for steak tonight?" Notice in my example, I didn't just say, "I would like steak". I added some details that informed him that steak would really lead to my happiness tonight, because I really have been craving it! Wahoo! Now the guy knows this is more than just a passing comment. It's an opportunity to win with you. Are you getting it?

Now, if you have not expressed what you want, and your man does something for you that isn't your cup of tea, be mindful of your own reaction. Do you think, "Wow, that was really generous, but I wasn't into it"? Maybe your man won't take you to a boxing match like mine was going to, but maybe he was excited about an evening he planned that wound up being something you didn't enjoy. Pay attention to how he reacts when you say, "I love that you went to all this trouble, but I have to tell you, I am not a fan of (fill in the blank)." There is no better time to get a man's attention than in the beginning when he is smitten with you and all about showing off to you.

I'll conclude this section by reiterating, because this really is one of the most important relationship lessons you could ever learn:

A man in love will demonstrate a powerful ambition to discover your happiness and deliver it to you. That passion for your happiness is the most reliable clue you could hope for. If you test this out, don't be afraid you are being self-indulgent. You are simply engaged in the process of discovering if he is the one!

Betray this rule and you won't achieve a relationship that is based on mutual love, devotion, respect, equity, honor and happiness. Sure, you can find love with a man, but it will eventually become an unfulfilling situation where the man leads the relationship focused on his own male-inspired recipe for how relationships should go. If you want to know what that looks like, look to your past, or imagine a relationship wherein you have to do everything for yourself, and he refuses to go to parties, see movies, or engage in activities that you are interested in. And it's all because you started and steered the relationship into a state where your happiness is not important.

On that note, make up your mind to steer the relationship in a way that considers his happiness as much as yours. Trust that under your guidance, both you and your partner will be equally treasured and pleased.

Embrace Your Standards Early

Most women, unbeknownst to themselves, are actually training men to take them for granted. You yourself won't recognize it because we were trained by generations of women before us that what men want is for us to take care of them and put our needs on the back burner, or ignore them entirely. There are many extreme examples of this out there, like cultures that encourage their women to be submissive and suppress all their needs so they are solely devoted to taking care of men. Then there are women who believe their man will learn to love her if she proves how easy it is to be with her. Easy = making no demands and having no needs. A woman like this tends to start off the relationship by suppressing her date's offers to do something for her by saying things like, "You choose," or, "No thanks, I don't need anything," or, "No, let me get it." When a man asks, "What would you like to do tonight?" and you reply, "I don't care," you are immediately starting a pattern of being invisible.

There are plenty of couples out there that are happy with this arrangement, and maybe you are one of them. But, if you have ever felt ignored, taken for granted, alone in a relationship, or even angry at men for their cluelessness, then you won't like that type of arrangement. You will want a man that follows the "devoted to your happiness" model. Trust me, this is not a manipulation, but instead is a fulfillment of what brings men satisfaction. So your job is to determine if the guy you are ga-ga for is on a quest for your happiness, or for making himself the center of your universe.

So the new standard is: Provide men with the information they need to know to make you happy! Being authentic and offering choices of what you genuinely would like to eat is an act of generosity, because making you happy makes him happy. Furthermore, it sets the tone that you matter and you are willing to have your needs and pleasures set the tone of the relationship.

With men, communication in which he does not have to guess is great. And when it's information that leads to your happiness, you've got his full attention. Unless of course you started off your relationship being "undemanding" and passive, and therefore, taught him that he does not have to work to win with you. He simply learns he does not even have to stretch to win for you, because you never seemed to care. Yes, you are so low maintenance, that some day, he will be excited by a woman that does care, and feels alive to be with her.

And, while he might still love you, he loves feeling wanted and inspired to WIN for her as well. This, my friend, is a recipe for a relationship that loses passion, intimacy and connection. I promise you, this point is really the key to how to have a relationship that does not grow apart. And this standard has to start at the onset! Trying to insert it later, after years of low expectations will be hard to make happen. So, please start this new standard early, and learn to maintain it!

Of course I am not suggesting you become a demanding, self-absorbed princess, but instead, recognize that giving your man the opportunity to be your provider of pleasure will keep a relationship fresh, and ensure that he will always look at you with love in his eyes. Why? Because you gave him something he always wanted but did not know was possible: A happy woman.

He is Interested in You...

Is That a Reason to Quit Dating Other Men?

Raising your bar involves no longer limiting your options simply because you think there are not enough great guys out there. You are meant to be with a guy who adores you, respects you and thrills in your happiness. Accept it!

Settling for less is easy when you think that a man is "the one" just because he's interested in you and he showed up in your life. Plenty of women plunge headlong into relationships because they think the guy was "sent to them" and it was "meant" to be, just because he's there. Don't make such life consuming choices so early. At first, a new guy is just a new option. Nothing more. You need time to determine if he has the qualities and the values you identify in your map. You need your list, and you need to know how he scores on that list, unless you are still into the idea of gambling your future on chance alone (but I hope you're past that by now!)

So how do you keep from getting stuck early in a relationship that started off well, but eventually revealed that he was not the one? An ounce of prevention is worth a pound of cure, as they say! When you

> "Date more than one man, so you don't get attached too early"

are in the 1st Gear of dating, see more than one person! **1st Gear is where you are having fun and learning if you have compatible interests** with the men you are seeing, but it's way too early to start heavier questions, like how he feels about kids and fidelity. 1st Gear is playtime. Give yourself the freedom to keep your own schedule and fill that schedule with activities that are fun for you. Remember step two? Be fully engaged while on your date, and be busy enough on your own time that you aren't waiting by the phone. You don't look for his text messages or emails, because you are busy. And you are busy with other dates as well, until you have given yourself ample time to let this man demonstrate that he is really into you (and for the right reasons)!

He Does Not Bring Out the Best in You

Here's another lesson involved with raising your bar. Have you ever been in a relationship that seemed to have great potential until you discovered that his personality or his approach to the relationship seemed to bring out the fight in you? You could be with one guy who tells you that you are too needy, but then when you find Mr. Right, he turns out to be more attentive, and with him, neediness just isn't an issue because he brings out the best in you. Sometimes "neediness" is just a mismatch in your desired level for attention" and in how much attention he feels he is willing to give anyone. You may need more attention than a certain guy can provide, but with another, his attention is juuuust right, so with him you are not considered needy.

Back to mismatches, you may even experience an extreme situation where you find yourself being abusive when it's against your nature. Perhaps his demeanor brings out the worst in you, and you are so frustrated that he won't listen to you that you find yourself complaining, arguing, or yelling too much. If that is truly out of character for you, perhaps it's time you recognize this personality type is not good for you. When a partner brings out the best in you, you'll find that you feel safe, respected, loved and you will grow until both of you discover the best in you!

Your Approach to Life is Different

Why be with a person who operates in life in a way that is the opposite of you? For instance, you are social and he hates being around people. He is closed off to communication and you have a strong need to talk about things with a partner. He likes to spend all his free time pursuing his hobbies and you want a family man who likes to spend time doing things with you. He likes to party and you don't. He's a slob and you are a neat freak. I am sure when I list polar opposite qualities like this; it's obvious that these two people are not compatible. Yet look into your past experiences and think about when you have been in a relationship where things fell apart because of irreconcilable differences. Again you hear the old "opposites attract" message. Well, some opposing behaviors do bring out the best in two people, but sometimes they don't, and you will find that a relationship rife with conflict brings out the worst in you. If that happens, move on! Especially before you make the foolish decision to forge ahead, try to make it work, and get married. A great relationship is one in which each partner respects and brings out the best in the other. Even if a great relationship is not your goal, at least be with someone whose life choices are mostly harmonious with yours.

Raise Your Bar About a Woman's Role in Relationships

If you carefully observe situations where one partner dominates the other for a one-sided relationship, you'll find that the dominant person is winning and the other is suppressed. But, a relationship built on mutual love and respect that takes both partner's needs into account has

"Steer the relationship in a way that considers his happiness as much as yours."

a strong foundation. And if you listen to 90% of the relationship experts out there today, they will tell you that women are the source for guiding men to great partnerships. Women, who realize this, can accept the role of master of their relation-SHIP!

Recently, I had a conversation with a client who could not get her man motivated to get a job. He had been out of work for at least 2 years. Her approach was to try to inspire him to want to be more proactive about looking for a job. She would dangle ideas about how it would improve his life, kindly pointing out the benefits, the pros and cons, and various logistical considerations. But she never pointed out the most important reason of all, which was that it was important to her; that she was suffering, or worse, losing respect for him! She was burdened by the thought of a future where she was going to have to work well beyond a reasonable retirement age, just because she was in love with a partner that would not see how important it was to her that he handle this now.

My advice to her was to stop trying to artfully paint these pictures in an effort to persuade him to change his values, because the truth was that he hadn't acted on her urging because this quality on her A list was not one he possessed! In a situation like that, you should use the strongest motivation that a woman has with a man: "The need to take care of you and make sure you are happy." His ability to do so is a measure of how good a partner he is. So when a man just isn't hearing you and you find yourself nagging, it's because you have failed to show him how you really need this from him, from a happiness and security perspective.

Luckily, my client took my advice and changed her approach to simply baring her fear to her partner. She openly shared with him that she was scared of a future where she would feel trapped because of the time they were losing in the pursuit of their long-term financial security. She explained her feelings on the importance of earning money, investing and preparing for retirement now. And just like that, he had a new motivation. He was now going to work at providing and caring for his woman. In his mind, he had felt that since he had just enough money saved to pay for his bills now, there was no pressing need to get a job. Plus, he felt the time he had off was providing a great pleasure to her, because he was working on home improvement projects around the house. He never knew she was worried about the future.

In her particular situation, when I suggested what she needed to say, she did not know how to have that conversation. It was a foreign approach for her, so luckily for her, we had a coaching session to help her learn. She admitted that she would not have figured out how to do it without examples and role playing. (That is what coaching sessions can look like.)

Most women go through life trying to make things easier for men, or feeling afraid to say something that will cause him to shut down. But I am here to tell you, that **his desire to make you happy and take care of you** is something you can take to the bank. If that is missing, kick the guy to the curb! It's a clue that he does not love you! Or at least not the way you really want and deserve.

Step 4 Assignment

Write down eight ways that you can raise your bar. Use some of the examples I have given you, but delve deeper, and look at yourself with a deep and profound sense of self-respect. What other ways could you raise your bar, maybe having to do with the way you pick men, settle for less or start off relationships? Even list areas that you see are behaviors of his that are not compatible with yours, or that bring out the worst in you.

Start a list in your Journal and title it, "My New Standards for Great Love!"

Keep this list where you can review it every time you go on a date so you don't lose track of your new standards. Without the reminder, it would be so easy to fall back into old patterns!

Chapter 5

How to Tell if a Man is in Love

Step 5: Men in Love Signals

Here is a fun set of tools to use! We're back to the age old question: "How do I know if he is in love with me?" Well there are some really telltale signs a man is in love with you.

> A man not showing he is in love, doesn't mean he is the wrong guy. It could just be the wrong time.

Correction, there are some specific signs that tell you if a man is in love in a healthy way. I'll provide you with a list first, then I will explain further.

Let's Start With the Early Stage of the Romance - aka 2nd and 3rd Gear.

1. He's eager to please you.
2. He pays close attention to what you say, looking for clues about what will make you happy and what he can do to please you.
3. He wants to know what you want to do, because he wants you to be happy.
4. He'll really be engaged in doing fun things to keep your attention and happiness.
5. He'll do things for you that he typically wouldn't do.
6. He is especially attentive towards your concerns, feelings, likes and dislikes.
7. When you say what you want, he's all ears.
8. Your safety, comfort and well-being matter to him.
9. He rolls with your "woman" nature.
10. He cares when you are upset.
11. He's likes to spend money on you and give up his time for you.

12. He'll spend time doing what you want, while putting his other activities on hold, or engaging in them less than normal.
13. He calls more frequently than is typical for him.
14. He often utters this expression, "Whatever makes you happy," or, "I just want you to be happy."
15. He'll listen to you prattle on about women's conversations that normally would bore him to death.

How does this list change once you are in 4th gear, which is when it is clear that he has won you over and now it's back to normal life? In other words, the courting is complete, he has moved on to being the provider, earner or just resumes the usual things he does with his time because he's no longer consumed with earning your love. It's not a bad thing. It's just that he can't continue to sacrifice his attention on taking care of business as much anymore. It's not productive for him to stay in courtship mode.

Let's Enter the Same List, and See How it Adjusts or Changes.

On the next page is a comparison of how his focus and actions shift when he is in 4th gear. Included are suggestions on how you can steer the relationship to stay fresh. Since he achieved something good and solid with you, he naively forgets the need for maintenance. Courting you and solidifying the relationship is similar to a completed task. It's natural for men to focus on being productive, and it's up to you to keep him engaged and present to maintain a healthy attention to the relationship. However, you must not over-shadow his need to get back to things that matter to him in life.

Below, the bolded words reflect his "back to production mode" behavior.

1. He can't do enough to please you. **He's still interested, but it's less overt.**
2. He pays close attention to what you say, looking for clues about what will make you happy and what he can do to please you. **Again, his attention seems to be more on "resuming life mode".**
3. He wants to know what you want to do, because he wants you to be happy. **He still does, so don't foul it up by always acquiescing to what he wants ("always" being the operative word)!**
4. He'll really be engaged in doing fun things to keep your attention and happiness. **Now we're downshifting to a more manageable schedule, like once or twice a week. After all, the rest of the time he has to play catch up on all the things he put on hold while courting you!**
5. He'll do things for you that he typically wouldn't do. **If you are smart, this will continue. But if you give in to his resistance because you want to make everything as easy on him as possible, you are ruining the rest of your life together! It is likely that you will lose him to his own self-satisfying comforts.**
6. He is especially attentive towards your concerns, feelings, likes and dislikes. **This is still true, but you have to first get his attention, and choose the right time.**
7. When you say what you want, he's all ears. **Still true! However you have to learn how to master the four rules of having a man hear what you want.**
8. Your safety, comfort and well-being matter to him. **Still true! (As long as you don't create an excessive pattern of complaining, in which case he will tune you out like how Charlie**

Brown hears his teacher or mom. "Wha wha wha, wha wha!")

9. He rolls with your "woman" nature. **Still very true! Your happiness and well-being are his main concern, and that won't die unless you kill it off by being one-sided (all complaints, and no happiness)!**

10. He cares when you are upset. **True, true, true. But when it sounds trivial, he will tune it out as typical "woman noise"!**

11. He's likes to spend money on you and give up his time for you. **Depends on the man. However, when a man goes back to business as usual, he often won't continue doing these things unless you show him that the things you want will contribute to your happiness!**

12. He'll spend time doing what you want, while putting his other activities on hold, or engaging in them less than normal. **Not! Like I said before, courting is over and now it's back to normal life. (Unless you cleverly keep him engaged.)**

13. He calls more frequently than is normal for him. **He calls as much as is necessary to make you happy, but again, taking care of life is now a priority. For a man, this equates to being a provider! If he did not have much of a life before you, you probably won't see much of a change. If he is the kind of guy who prizes his activities more than your happiness, you will see a radical change in his attentiveness.**

14. He often utters this expression, "Whatever makes you happy," or, "I just want you to be happy." **This won't change for the rest of your life. Even if you part company, he will always tell you that this mattered to him. If not, then he never loved you in the first place. At least not in the way you deserve.**

15. He'll listen to you prattle on about women's

conversations that normally would bore him to death. **He'll pretend, but you'll know he is zoned out. The antidote for zoning out is getting his attention. Again, the four rules for helping a man hear you must be mastered. At this point in your new growth, it's too early to teach you that lesson.**

Understanding Men

There are a few basics you want to know about men in love. Once a man loves you, it is hard to lose his love. The only behaviors that would destroy it for him are two things...

> ➢ Your happiness is unattainable for him!
> ➢ He can't win with you!

Some of you may still not understand what this means, even at this point. If that is true, then quick! Take every course, every teleseminar, and listen to every taped discussion on the topic, because those two statements are the keys to the kingdom.

Once you really understand both the simplicity, and the importance of those statements, you will discover a man that is devoted to you for the rest of your life. You will have a relationship that others thought only existed in fairy tales, because they could not imagine what a deeply and persistently happy partnership looked like.

I am not suggesting life will always be singing happy tunes, but when you hone this tremendous talent for honoring what really matters to men (again the two simple rules I just gave you), then your guy will go through anything with you, including the darkest days of your life. Even when you don't seem to be able to generate joy or attentiveness to anyone or anything because you are so overwhelmed, he'll be there with you. Why is that? Because you exposed him to something that **he did not know was possible but always dreamed of: A happy woman!**

You don't have to worry about losing a man in love! He is in love! And for most men, that's it!

This is why, when a man decides he is in love; real, deep and unequivocal love; he will stick by your side until the end of time. Men are different that way (at least the healthy men are). Nothing but a constant, unrelenting feeling of failure with you will kill off that love. Not even divorce or time apart.

Where Women Ruin a Man's Love and Attention

As children, some of us learned from our mothers not to bother dad. We internalize that statement (intended for a child who can't comprehend that it just isn't a good time) and interpret its meaning as: Men don't like to be bothered by a woman's needs. The mischief here is that when you grew up, no one ever told you that statement was only intended for a little girl, but as a woman, you are entitled to a new rule.

The new rule is to communicate whatever needs and wants will maintain the happiness of the courtship/honeymoon phase of your relationship. He wants you to be happy, but he also wants you to bring these things up when it's a good time. Also, for the best success, you should make sure that you really have his full attention and focus for the important things you want to communicate to him.

If the little girl tape in your head tells you not to bother men and that he'll be happier if you never need or want anything from him, you will set a pattern where he will never feel that he should do anything for you. As the years go on like this, you'll probably notice that he doesn't even listen to you anymore, and he won't go with you to chick flicks, classes or parties, simply because you started the relationship by not bothering him as a way of showing your love!

The secret to a good, lasting relationship is to never lose sight of the fact that you should **keep a man on his toes by always setting your happiness bar just high enough that he never takes you for granted**. Don't think of this as teasing him. Think of it as a way to keep the relationship a priority for him while giving him something to pursue! That's what men live for!

You know that proverbial "chase" that people speak of? That is what you create for him when you sweetly, playfully keep your man on his toes in the pursuit of your happiness!

Step 5 Assignment

Write down three inspirations you received from this chapter, and then share your insights with at least two other women, preferably more. The more you talk about it with positive energy, the sooner it will ultimately result in burning the message into your psyche, making you believe. If you are like me, and you share this message every week, it not only becomes part of your thinking, but it will change the way men react to you. Suddenly, not only will you see more appealing men, but they will be automatically attracted to you!
Step 6: Let Go of Him to Move on!

Step 6:   Let Go of The Relationship That Still Haunts You

I know from first-hand experience how hard it is to let go of an old love that ended feeling incomplete. When that happens, are you still hooked? If you are still carrying on feelings of upset ,or if you simply repeat the stings of past injustices over and over in your mind, then this chapter pertains to you!

- Do you feel that you are open to new love coming into your life, even though you still feel that "hook" in your heart?

- Have you stopped dating altogether, feeling consumed by the thoughts that riddle your mind?
- Do you date endlessly, but it never leads to anything because no one measures up?
- Do you feel incomplete, but still put yourself out there, hoping that some guy will overwrite this pain and show you that you are worthy of love?
- Do you find your anger consuming you, or every day you think about him?

If you answered yes to any of the above scenarios, then I suggest you recognize the power this unresolved love has on your heart and your mind, because it will interfere with the choosing of the right guy in the future!

Here are ways that this old hook in your heart can interfere with your ability to pick a man who has the potential to be the love of your life:

- Your mind and heart are wounded and not really open
- You compare every new guy to Mr. X.
- You go on dates but no one measures up.
- You are even picky about how you will date, which is why you are not dating.
- You feel diminished by the opinion of your ex, and this affects any new relationship.
- You are still trying to prove your ex wrong in your mind or in the process of dating.
- You are sending out a message on dates that you don't trust men.
- You are starting off dating like it's an inquisition, asking entirely too many questions before it's appropriate to ask.
- You talk about your ex too much on dates.
- You overreact to men's behaviors.
- You bash men a lot and don't see why that is wrong.

> If you can't let go of a past love, rate him through your map.

If you answered yes to any of the above statements, then you are hooked, whether you can admit it to yourself or not. Furthermore, these residual feelings are influencing your judgment, openness and dating patterns. Avoiding this inquiry will just come back to bite you. This baggage is large, and will wind up more like a wall if not dealt with. I have observed over and over that when you can properly let go of an unresolved, hurtful relationship, you will experience a sudden sensation of freedom and weightlessness, like a switch got flipped, allowing all the possibilities of great love to flow through you.

To help you let go, you need clarity on what went wrong. Did you build your entire relationship around one or two traits that you loved? Did you simply get caught up in the intoxicating feeling of love that came with the inexplicable sense that you were both completely happy and connected? Well there actually is an explanation for that wild delirium. It's called dopamine, but I refer to it as "The Love Drug". It's so powerful that it can cloud your judgment completely, and stimulate an overwhelming feeling of love, even when not much has been offered to substantiate such intensity of emotion. That's why people think the relationship is "magic", or "meant to be", or "written in the stars" among other nebulous explanations. The term "Love Drug" is particularly apt, because on top of its ability to change reality, some people chase its effects for a lifetime, like addicts that don't know they are addicts! To break the "spell" of the not-so-magical dopamine, simply focus on the list, and remind yourself over and over that he was really not enough for you, and he never will be. Don't think he will change. The truth is that he is not motivated to change, and only **you** are hurting yourself by not moving on. You have a choice to suffer and waste your life, or recognize that the hurt is paralyzing you and that only you can choose to move on and let go.

The reality is that trying to win him back, or prove to him that you are worthy will never work. He does not possess the qualities you need in a mate. It doesn't make him a bastard or a jerk; it just means he does not want the same things you want. Truth! He could never make you happy! So any more time wasted on him is stealing time from your life. The all-consuming pursuit to prove your value to him or to change his mind will only delay you from discovering the incredible man out there who is waiting eagerly to love you the way you deserve to be loved!

Think of that failed relationship as a lesson; simply a learning experience to help you grow! It wasn't about torturing you or hurting you, but about helping to show you what works for you and what doesn't. The fact that it was painful or unsatisfactory is exactly what it should have been, because when you finally look at your SoulMate Map©, you will be able to see that you were simply not compatible.

Let him go, and let go of your need to prove something! There is no cheese down that tunnel. He will never fit with you! It's even possible that he really does love you, in his own way, or did. But his way won't make you happy; can't possibly make you happy, because he is missing compatible partnership traits! That's the answer! Of all the 10 steps in this process, I think this particular step, more than any other, requires you to get another person to help you with their objective set of eyes. Whatever you do, don't talk with a friend who will just say what they think you want to hear. That would be a disaster. Instead, choose someone who can be kind, yet powerfully direct in their observations and suggestions, and who can help to reinforce your certainty that this guy did not match your SoulMate Map©, and that you are better off without him!

If you are still having trouble letting go, then I highly recommend you work with an expert to help you, particularly if this is in the way of you finding love. Not addressing this unresolved conflict could result in 10, 15, or 20 years of 'Broken Picker' experiences.

Step 6 Assignment:

What measures are you going to take to let go of that unhealthy man? **The voice in your head that repeats what you love about him is what keeps you trapped.** Therefore, the way to reverse engineer your thinking is to replace those one or two traits you love about him, make a list of the ways that he disappointed you or continuously failed you. It's time to free yourself up to pursue love that is worthy of you. Any time you find yourself missing him or wishing he loved you more, simply read **his failure list over and over, till you feel you've gotten your mind back to clarity**.

Chapter 6

Are You Compatible as Partners?

Step 7:   What is Your Partnership Model?

Now it's time to learn how to find a lasting soul mate based on matched and compatible partnership styles. People tend to be somewhat mystified about the idea of "partnership styles," and if you are one of those people, the following should provide you with some clarity.

If I were to ask you to come up with a list of ten couples whose relationships you admire, how many do you think you could find? Some of you might have a hard time listing five; some even less. Great marriages are those based on **partnership**, not just civility or looking good for the Joneses. So let's dig beneath the surface.

What qualities do you think make a great partnership? This is such an important factor in solid relationships that can withstand the ups and downs of life through the years. Matching approaches to partnership will ensure that you can work together, argue successfully, resolve conflicts without killing each other, and find unification on how you spend money, handle parenting, create passion, have fun and maintain intimacy.

One issue that causes couples to fail is that they have different ideas about their roles as partners. In fact, most of the time people aren't even conscious of their own expectations! These things are rarely discussed in advance. It's just assumed that everyone thinks and feels the same way about partnership roles and partnership agreements. This lack

> If you don't have your own partnership model, you end up being lead by the one who does.

of understanding leads scads of couples into fights, arguments and unresolved break-downs.

So how to avoid this? The key here is communication. Most people don't really verbalize what their partnership style is because they haven't given it much thought. As I mentioned earlier, the whole subject is largely unconscious. Being aware of what makes a great partnership is paramount so you'll know how to figure out whether you are a match through communication.

Let's take my marriage for an example of partnership model compatibility. From the beginning, we began developing a strong relationship model based on an agreement that we would always put the partnership first over our individual needs. This allowed us to persevere through the first years of marriage, during which, as with every relationship between two individuals, we had to figure out

> Matched and compatible partnership style is the secret to our marriage.
> - Denise Culley

how to reconcile our differences in communication and the way we handled things. We discovered that our partnership model really helped us to face the hard conversations, or make choices that were essential for keeping the partnership solid when it would have been easier for me to just do what I wanted or for him to do what he wanted. Even at those times when I feel I am right and he is wrong, I remind myself of our partnership agreement and that immediately snaps me out of it. Sometimes I have to swallow my need to be right for the good of the partnership. It's like they say. The whole is greater than the sum of its parts! Our mutual dedication to our partnership model keeps each of us from making purchases regardless of our partner's feelings or our budget. It allows us to talk openly, respectfully and without fear of retribution. It includes our agreement about fidelity as well as the freedom to look without fear of jealousy. I can't tell you how many times each of us came back after an argument and quickly resolved our upsets because we both honored our partnership model.

Here is my challenge for you. First of all, if you don't have a partnership model, then you will absolutely, without a doubt, have havoc in your relationship. However, if you don't have any idea of what you need and want in a partnership, then you will naturally wind up conforming to whatever his model is. I think it is important to point out here that I have yet to see a partnership model work if it was exclusively designed by the man.

Don't ignore what is important to you! Take the time now to figure out what you want in a partnership! Let's talk about the influence of parents, which can largely set your expectations for what a partnership should look like.

Your mom and dad had their model for partnership. If they fought a lot, it was because they came from families with opposing partnership models and unwittingly or unconsciously adopted their parents' model automatically by default. What if your future husband/life partner came from parents that believed that sweeping problems under the rug was the way to deal with things, and you came from a family where you talked things out? What if you did not know this in advance? I'll tell you. After the rosy period of your relationship gives way to life's circumstances, you would be faced with the jarring realization that you can't work together on a resolution.

What if you came from a family where the woman rules the home and you take after that model? Then you chose a guy who feels that he would be a wimp if he let the woman make the decisions. That's an instant recipe for warfare and total breakdown in partnership.

So how to prevent this? Let's get back to the key of communication that I mentioned earlier. The smart and simple course of action would be to have discussions before you get to a commitment stage of the relationship, which I call 3rd Gear. Having this conversation too early in the dating/relationship process is a relationship killer. If you talk about this too soon, you will usually frighten a man away. The truth is, to be able to have this conversation at the right time will take some forethought on your part. The more you become acquainted with your own values and partnership needs, the stronger your relationship will be. That's because you will be honoring yourself and your standards, which is essential for a happy partnership. As with most women, it will probably help you to know that your clarity about your role in a partnership is inviting and reassuring to men. It all goes back to the happiness model.

This subject is far too vast to be fully explored in this introductory exercise, but it's a start. It's a new awareness that you must establish now so you can attract a man who will be a great partner. Great relationships are the result of great partnerships!

Take the time to really dig deep as you answer all the questions below. This is a crucial step in your SoulMate Map© development and will greatly improve your results. Compatibility depends not only on having the same model for partnerships, but also for romance, communication, relationship roles, intimacy, and how you handle conflicts.

Step 7 Assignment

Think about and identify the partnership model that you grew up with. Which aspects of that model do you want to keep and which do you want to exchange for something you think would be a better way of handling things? Pay attention to couples who have relationships that you admire. Ask them what they think makes their partnership work. Specifically ask them about partnership, because this exercise is not just about compatibility. It's how you will work together as a team.

Here are some categories I have expanded on to help get you started with isolating elements of partnership that are important to you. Write them down in your journal.

Love

How do you express love? Verbally? Physically? Do you like to talk about your feelings? Do you show love by doing things for your partner? Do you feel that talking about your feelings is over rated? Do you think that it's unnecessary to say, "I love you," because the fact you are faithful or committed to the relationship should make it clear? Do you need to hear, "I love you," from your partner? Do you like to be acknowledged? Do you like to give acknowledgment? Are you huggy-feely? Do you express love through intimate touch? Do you feel uncomfortable hugging or touching? Do you express love through intimate discussions? Do you like to cuddle? Do you like to kiss? How important is kissing to you? How important is sex to you? Is sex not a priority to you? Do you like to flirt? Do you like to be touched or stroked? Do you like/need massages? Do you like to give massages? Do you like to touch your partner?

Conflicts

Do you like to talk things out when troubles arise? Do you like time to think before discussing? Are conversations about conflicts too confrontational for you? Do you have aversions to conflicts because of fights you experienced in your past? Have you been taught from childhood that hitting is a form of love? Do you argue when you run into differences in opinions? Do you yell? Are you hot tempered? Do you get loud when you get passionate? Are you impatient? Do you hate to have your partner walk away from you when you have a fight or disagreement? Do you find you can't speak when your partner is upset? Do you feel suppressed from thinking or saying anything because you were never allowed to voice your feelings growing up? Did you resent one of your parents for being weak and succumbing to their partner when they had conflicts? Did you resent one of your parents for being dominating to their partner? Do you just give in to avoid fighting at all costs? Do you think that couples should not fight? Do you run away from conflicts or upsets?

Sharing Responsibilities

I could not possibly list enough questions on this subject, so you will need to come up with most of the list on your own. I will just get you started.

Do you feel that chores should be divided and each partner should take care of their areas of responsibility? Do you feel everyone should chip in and do whatever needs to be done? Do you think each person should be responsible for themselves? Do you feel that if one person makes more money, the other person should do more at home? Do you tend to take on the house chores as your responsibilities because you are a woman? Do you tend to be in relationships with men that don't do their share at home? What describes your style and comfort zone for the following areas: Who pays the bills? Who does the food shopping? Who cooks the food? Who plans the vacations?

Parenting

Whether you are hoping to find a mate to start a family with, or you have a family and want a partner that will be just as compatible with your kids as he is with you, this last list will help you to be conscious to the parenting styles or expectations that one might have, but never verbalize.

With an existing family

Do you expect him to be an active partner with your kids, or do you want him to respect that you are the parent, and he needs to defer to you for parenting.

Or maybe you want him to be active. A good question to answer might be is whether you are a disciplinarian, or are you more indulgent.

New parents

If you don't have a family and plan to create a family with him, you'll want to list your expectations on how you would partner in your parenting approach and what you expect of him.

I'm not an expert about parenting, so I can't offer any advice. I trust you can come up with a list on your own.

To inspire you to come up with a good list, I'll tell you a couple of stories.

When I was in my twenties, I was not sure whether to start a family or not. Thank goodness I had a conversation with my husband at the time. He said something that was a deal killer for me. He said "it's up to you, since you are the one who will be raising the kids".

This came as a shock to me, because I thought he loved kids. After all, when we were around friends, he would play with their kids. Hearing that he felt I would be more involved with the kids than him set off a warning signal to me. It's a good thing we had that conversation. We didn't start a family and that turned out to be a good thing, since we actually divorced two years later.

Later on in life, I met a man who had a child from a former relationship. I won't bore you with all the details, however, seeing him with his kid caused me to lose respect for him and ultimately fall out of love.

If you are stuck for ideas, talk to friends and family, Observe friends, and jot down what you appreciate or dislike about your friends' styles. Of course, you don't want to record the negative attributes in your list, so to use your thoughts about what you want to avoid, you can record them by entering a trait that would offset the negative parenting style.

Some questions you might need answered:

How many children do you want? Who takes care of the kids? Who is the primary caretaker? What style of discipline do you use for parenting? Do you like to buy your children every convenience in life or do you believe in setting limits on how many gifts they get? How do you plan to teach them lessons about earning things? Do you believe in assigning chores to your kids? What are your rules about how your child earns or receives allowances? Do you even believe in giving allowances?

Since I am not an expert on parenting, I'm leaving it up to you to come up with a robust list of issues for you to consider. However, you can look at your own childhood, recall what values and rules you had, and decide which ones you want to replicate and which ones you strongly want to avoid.

Another great source for parenting ideas can be found on Wikipedia. Simply Google "parenting style", and look for the Wiki page.

Add all these categories to your journal on all these categories (and any you might have come up with) as new thoughts occur to you over time

Chapter 7

The Advantage of a SoulMate Map

Now it's time to prepare you for create your
SoulMate Map©· In the next chapter you will start creating
your lists. You will be guided to discover answers for ten
topics which were cleverly designed to reveal more about
you, than what you are looking for in a mate. The reason
for concentrating on you is that we want someone to
match **your** core values and approach to life. The goal is
compatibility as a partner. However this will be created in
a way that will reveal more than you would create on your
own. Therefore, be open, mindful and approach this from
trust. Trust in that many women before you have
discovered that this approach works.

After you've created all the lists, you will then go back
and review them and identify which of the traits and
qualities are more important than others. But, don't worry
about that now. Instructions will be provided later when
it's time to think about it.

The ultimate goal is to come up with a compatibility list
you can count on.

Your Lists Becomes Your Compatibility List

Have you ever been accused of being too selective?
Or perhaps your M.O. is just the opposite; you are not
selective at all. Or perhaps your method for selection is
based on gut and chemistry alone. The A list will become
a better guide or formula for evaluating whether your new
love interest will be a long lasting partner.

What is an "A" list? The A list is the end game. This is
basically your compatibility list. After identifying the
qualities in each of the ten lists, you will have a very

lengthy list. Later on we'll guide you to paring it down to a more concise A list, and will help you gain more clarity as to which of these qualities are essential to a long lasting relationship with a highly compatible partner. Every person's A list will be different. Sure, some specific qualities should be on everyone's A list, such as love and respect. Therefore the items that you'll tag as "A" are the qualities you deem as "must have". These are the things you need to know about your man before committing to a relationship.

If you are currently in a relationship, and well on the way to commitment, take a good hard look, because if your partner is missing most of the items in your "must have" list, you are going to struggle, and you have less than a 50/50 chance of survival. If I was a Love Doctor, I would tell you that your prognosis is grim. However, if your man has most of what is on your A list, you have a strong foundation for working everything out, as long as you learn how to communicate, maintain a solid partnership commitment, and accept your role as "Man Whisperer". A Man Whisperer is a woman who knows that her role is to guide a man to success as a partner by cleverly teaching him what he needs to know to make the partnership work.

Assuming he knows how to be a great partner to you, or expecting him to "read your mind", in your relationship is living on fantasy island and will blow up one day. Your A list will help you to know what is important to you and what you potentially will need to work on. But you should know, because you have allocated these things as "Must Haves", you need to honor yourself and take a stand that you will do whatever you can to convey what you want and need in a relationship.

If You Are Single and Not Yet Dating

Use the SoulMate Map© to give you the confidence that you will know whether a man is worth your time! But this statement comes with a strong warning. Do NOT try to figure out if he matches your map in the beginning of your dating experience. I am referring to the period that is just the 1st Gear, when you first meet and go out on dates to find out if you are attracted to each other and if you can have <u>fun</u>. Tragically, women who grill a man to find out how he thinks and feels about certain traits, goals and items on her A list, on the first few dates are destroying the whole art of dating. Holy camolly! What a turn-off! The average man would run for the hills when a woman starts with this type of investigation right off the bat! There is plenty of time for the serious conversations later. Allow it to come forth in 2nd Gear, when it's apparent that you have chosen to date each other exclusively. Then make sure you get all these answers in the 3rd Gear of dating, when it's the time to discuss and discover whether you are serious about partnership and commitment.

If you enter into an engagement or cohabitation arrangement, without knowing whether your guy matches your "A" list, it will be like walking into a house that has traps and hazards you can't see because you have a blindfold on. Your feelings alone can't tell you if a guy is the one! You could love a man to pieces, but that does not mean he is meant to be your life partner, or that your love can endure the typical challenges of any relationship.

You want to enter a relationship with your eyes wide open to the knowledge that while he might not be perfect in every way, he's a match on the core beliefs and values that can bond you deeply as a couple. A relationship built on that kind of compatibility will give you a sense of deep and profound love that transcends anything you have ever imagined.

Cautions

If you feel that being physically fit is a "must have," I can get that, but remember a person's physical appearance will change in time. Perhaps what you are more interested in is how they live their life in terms of health, fitness, and maintaining a healthy body. Therefore, I recommend you curb your focus on physical traits in your A list, and instead focus on the lifestyle or values that supports him being someone you would be attracted to. If you enter "green eyes" as one of your "must haves", then don't blame the process for the fact that you are still out there looking. Don't be a "Don Quixote" who is always chasing the impossible dream.

Other Unexpected Benefits:

Your Map Mirrors You!

I've heard from women that the unexpected benefit for them was that they discovered themselves in this process. In fact, one of the women suggested that I include a chapter about it, because in her experience, she found new self-esteem while mapping for a soul mate.

I'd like to also include a review from a long distance client, This was from her Amazon book review. I think it says it better than I could write.

A Treasure Map...and you are the treasure!

I just wanted to share about what this book has done for me, personally! I am at the tail end of a divorce and am also a single mother of a four and a half year old.

I married a man at a time when my self-esteem was low and I felt I needed rescuing. I finally took the steps to get a divorce, which I feel empowered by, but the divorce left me with doubt and trust issues about my ability to choose men wisely.

SoulMate Map gave me a new sense of encouragement and confidence. I am now empowered and inspired by love again! This is huge, because I was one who had pretty much given up on getting it right in the love department!

When I followed the steps in her "Map", it felt like I was going on a treasure hunt, and I was the first treasure to be found! I rediscovered my joys and passions...I re-discovered me!

You'll have the attractor factor working for you! Between the discoveries in your new SoulMate Map© and the things you will learn in the next section, you should be in the process of embracing some new revelations, and suddenly you will notice that men are finding you more attractive. Your former doubt is being replaced with a new awareness, and that is the source of your magnetism.

Confidence in dating! Armed with your map, you can relax and enjoy dating more, knowing that the time to figure out whether he is a match will come later.

Give "diamonds in the rough" a chance! One very special boost to your dating experience is that you will see men differently. Hopefully, your standards will have been raised, and your radar more fine-tuned. Men you typically wouldn't have given a chance before now, have an opportunity to shine for you. In the past, you could have met an extraordinary man, but since you were looking solely for whether you felt chemistry, you passed on him because you were looking through the wrong lens. Now you have your soul mate glasses on and working!

When I look back on my decisions about the men who became my significant others, and the ones I passed on, I can now see where I should have given the diamonds in the rough a chance, but acted unfairly, and where I should have let go so much quicker of those I now know were obviously never a match. But, my emotions were my primary guide back then, because I did not have a SoulMate Map© of my own.

The "Relatability" List

Most of your traits would probably fall into your "B" rating. While the "A"s are glaring evidence to tell you whether you should move on or stick with him, the "B"s represent potential. These list items are still very important. While "A" is where your safety and security lies, "B" is where your happiness lies. But the "B"s are also where the highs and lows, and the peaks and valleys of a relationship are created. Every relationship has them. Your B list is where the dance of partnership comes into play. It's totally up for negotiation, give and take. One year's B list could be altered by your own growth; new interests, new people in your life, etc.

Your B list could be what makes you unique or what makes your differences complement each other, like when opposites attract. It's all up to you, based on how serious or committed you are to your choices, or how open you are to change.

Your B list could be your lightning rod for a realization that you are not compatible, or it could be the catalyst for the intrigue that you offer each other.

Your B list could be your map for educating a man how to gain your attention or to please you. If a man learns your B list, he could use it as a way to keep romance and partnership alive. After all, it's loaded with information about what makes you happy. Didn't we say your happiness is a man's greatest desire?

This list may include interests and lifestyle choices that you wish to convince him are worthwhile. Just because someone does not match you 100% on your B list is not a reason to discard him as a soul mate. It just shows you where your challenges are and where you can potentially complement each other. It's an individual evaluation and a personal decision. Allow me to use myself as an example yet again!

On my A list I have, "love to travel". I need to have travel in my life. It's one of my top pursuits and areas for enjoyment and pleasure. It really is in my top ten goals in life. However, where I travel is on my B list.

The Final List is Small and Inconsequential

In comparison to the other items on your list, the "C"s aren't really important to you. You don't have to throw this set away, but if you won't date a guy because he is, does, or looks like something on your "C" list, then face facts: You are making this harder on yourself than is practical. It's a flag that you are not ready for dating/relationships. You have some fears and healing to take care of, and while I know you are conflicted and unhappy, just imagine how it feels for the poor unsuspecting guy who likes you, when he gets dumped once again by a woman for something trivial. For example, you don't like the way he dresses, or how he combs his hair.

To keep things in perspective, here is an example of something that is on my C list. I can't imagine dating a man that orders hamburgers in a Chinese restaurant. Can you even conceive of putting that on your A list? That means that all his other qualities are thrown out the window because you find cuisine choices a critical element for soul mate selection! Yeah, I know it sounds funny now, but as a relationship coach, I hear this kind of stuff come out of women's mouths all the time! They may not have listed something silly like this on their map, but when you hear them talk about why they won't go out on a second or third date, or why they are certain that a man should be nothing more than a friend, it has the ring of a flimsy reason not to give a man a chance to reveal his best side!

Men can be nervous about dating, and as a result, they might not shine their brightest. Or perhaps he is just a man who is clueless about what impresses women, what they like to talk about, etc. But please know, you can't judge all men in just a few dates. Some men are just as nervous as women about "acting the right way and saying the right things" on dates, and that nervous energy can make a lot of really great diamonds in the rough come off as losers with a capital L. So if that is your M.O., you are going to have to alter it if you expect to find someone fabulous. Not all guys have the skill to present their best attributes on a first or second date. Especially if he likes you and has the wrong notion about what impresses women. He might say or do something that is not his normal behavior. It might be something awkward he came up with during a nervous impulse. This is not necessarily a sign that he is not date-able or relationship worthy. It could just mean he is a diamond in the rough. Don't gave up on him before really finding out..

The moral of the story

Having a list is much better than just making snap judgments or comparisons. The map will keep you on your "A" game (pun intended) and help you to recognize sooner when a man is more than a challenge; that he is just flat out not compatible.

I am here as evidence, as a reformed women who used the wrong criteria for getting to know men and choosing those I thought were "the one". If I had continued on that path, I would never have chosen my dream husband. In fact, my instant opinion of him was that he was not my type. I was not attracted; I did not feel chemistry, etc. But instead of acting on my typical model for dating, I gave him a chance as a friend. He didn't give up, because he already felt there was something special about me. Only after being authentic and sharing what mattered to me did I get to know him better. Within 3 months, I had discovered he was a man that I could love and live with for the rest of my life! I felt it deeply, but in a grounded way. Not that frilly fairly tale way that makes you fluttery and befuddled like only chemicals in your brain can do. Now, years later, I feel a rich and wholly fulfilling love that I did not even know existed. It's incredible to be bonded in a partnership where your man has your back and you have his. My husband is very aware of what matters to me and what makes me happy and he listens to me. He gets me.

I never have to wonder if he will stray or betray me with infidelity, because like I told you, before we got married, I made it perfectly clear what was on my A list, so he has always honored my must-haves in life. Fidelity is definitely on my A list, and he won't compromise that because he knows it would break my heart and break me, and he is very much aware of the consequences of that. No matter what you may think about men, if they love you, they WON'T want to break your heart! Often, men think that if they don't get caught then there is no way of breaking your heart. The smart woman makes sure she is not shy about making him profoundly aware of how devastated she would be in that event. Having that conversation will raise his awareness and perhaps make him think twice before he ever allows something to develop.

My hope is that you are starting to see the many ways in which your SoulMate Map© will guide your choices, and even your partnership steering for years to come! It really is a map, isn't it?

Hope and Growth

I hope your bar has been raised, and your reality has been restored. When you can see relationships for what they truly are, and you are grounded by the knowledge that you have a list that tells you whether a man has the qualities you need, then you will naturally bring a new freedom and clarity to your dating.

I hope you will learn and grow from creating the lists in the following SoulMate Map©. You will radiate a new, irresistible force, and will discover that, without even trying, you have a new aura of attraction working for you. So don't be surprised by a big paradigm shift where interesting men are suddenly being attracted to you!

Are you ready to start your lists?

Before you get started on your list making, you have a decision to make. Do you want to create your list on your own, or would you like to benefit from a list compiled from other women whom have created their SoulMate Map© online?

Below is a special offer for women whom have bought this book.

A Special Online Gift from Denise!

Link to Gift: http://SoulMateMap.com/gift

Chapter 8
My Gift to You!

I have a gift for you! No it's not a man. It's a fun and fast way to create your SoulMate Map©. Before I tell you, let me start with some questions.

Let's Start by Pondering a Few Questions:

➢ Do you dislike making lists alone?

➢ Is it a challenge for you to come up with answers?

➢ Would you prefer to choose from a list of suggestions?

➢ Would you like advice from a Relationship coach, because it's too important to get your A list correct?

Most of the woman I have met personally, shared those concerns with me, which is why I am extending this gift to anyone reading this book.

Prefer to Get Some Help With Creating Your Lists?

Before we dive into the first list, let's talk about some things you should know to make sure you get the maximum benefit from the SoulMate Map©.

Because I am married to a web engineer, I am fortunate to be able to offer you the choice of working on your SoulMate Map© list exercises either manually (using paper and pen) or online.

I'd like to give you a little history about my insights regarding the creation of lists. I first released this book in 2011. What I noticed is that women loved the messages and lessons in the book, but **never sat down to work on their lists**. Which is sad really, because it really defeats my whole intention. How are women going to receive the full affect and insights that come from creating their SoulMate Map©, if they don't actually create one?

Finding out that most women never sat down to work on their lists gave me the idea to host a full day seminar to help women get their lists done in one day, in the company of other women. After all, the lessons I have provided for you so far are only half of the journey. To truly improve your broken picker, you need to be armed with your A list.

The A list is refined through a process. You will learn more about the process later. It can be daunting to come up with lists on your own. What I noticed is that when the women shared their lists with each other, they heard ideas and qualities that they wouldn't have thought of on their own.

Since I live in a small town in California and couldn't possibly travel to every town in America, let alone globally, I had to come up with something different. That's when I had the exciting idea to create an online process that mimics the experience of seeing other's lists.

Here are the benefits:

➢ Each list comes with its own set of suggested answers, collected from other women.

➢ It's so much quicker to complete, when you have examples. Less strain on your brain.

➢ You'll have a more complete A list, than you might have come up with on your own.

➢ You can still add traits and qualities that are specific to your needs and desires.

➤ You can work at your own pace.

➤ When it's time to grade and collect all of your A list attributes, the online program makes it easy for you.

➤ There are reports provided (at the end) for compatibility, and conversation starters.

➤ There's a section to compare your past or current men to your A list, next to a visual. How they do or do not match up is eye opening.

➤ With your permission I can review your lists, and provide some fine tuning recommendations, so you can have the best possible list.

➤ You never have to worry about misplacing your "A" list, because you can always find it online.

➤ The online SoulMate Map© is secure, and password protected. Your privacy matters to us.

Remember I said that your A list is your blueprint, meant to help you stay on track and avoid being fooled by either a player, a charmer, or simply someone who triggers your old broken picker patterns.

"To successfully find your soul mate, don't take short cuts, follow the process as they unfold"
– Denise Culley

You'll want to use the online SoulMate Map© if you say yes to any of the following:

➤ Your M.O. is to think the answers rather than writing them down.

➢ You believe in dream boards, and seeing your answers in print is a visual tool.

➢ You tend to do things your own way.

➢ You feel you don't have time to create your lists.

➢ You have so much going on, that even though you will have the best intention to create your lists, you will ultimately get distracted by something else, and forget.

➢ You've come up with compatibility lists before which only had 10 – 20 items listed.

➢ You don't believe in creating lists. (However, the outcome of this process will surprise and delight you.)

➢ You have a tendency to misplace lists.

➢ You are confronted by the idea of coming up with qualities you want in a mate.

➢ You don't want to do this alone.

The LISTS in this workbook are the real keys to success, so make sure you give them your all! To receive the full power and benefit of this process, **record your discoveries!**

Also, you should know that this workbook was designed with painstaking care and a high-level of specificity, so it is **incredibly important that you follow the process just as I've laid it out**. If you mix it up and do it your way, you are not following the SoulMate Map© process, so you can't expect the best results. For example, skipping a lesson will cut off the great success of doing it as instructed. I can't stress this enough. This process has been developed over years of client experience. Those that follow it correctly all report meeting and falling in love with the greatest partners they could ever dream of. So what you do is up to you, but we want you to find your best match possible, so please follow it as directed!

Now it's time to choose whether you want to continue using the workbook to create your SoulMate Map©, or if you want to go on-line...

Your SoulMate Map© Online

Here is a preview of how fun and easy the online program is:

Online SoulMate Map©

If you want to proceed to the online SoulMate Map©, simply use the URL below.

Copy this link on your computer, or tablet. (It won't work very well on a smart phone.)

http://SoulMateMap.com/workbook

Recommendation: In chapter nine there are instructions on how to create your SoulMate Map©. You could read the guidelines in the book first, or go to the online soul mate map workbook and read the guidelines as you work. Whichever you choose, please don't miss reading the instructions in this book.

Frequently Asked Questions:

Q: Will I need a login?

A: Yes, you will be asked to provide your email address so that you can receive a copy of the completed lists if you prefer. Also, to provide a secure login, you must first click on the confirmation link in the confirmation email. We don't want anyone invading your lists

Q: Will my info be private?

A: Yes, because you have a login, no one will be able to see your lists other than me. I only need to access your lists if you request coaching or answers to your questions. There is a comment section at the bottom of every list for asking questions or posting comments. The comments may be seen by others after I have reviewed them, so don't post anything private in the comment section. You can simply ask me to delete them after I read them privately.

Q: Do I need a computer?

A: You'll need a browser. This program is accessible using the internet (or WiFi) and a browser. Therefore you can view it on a desktop, laptop, or tablet. In some instances, if you have a browser on your eReader (Kindle, Nook or iBook) you can use your eReader.

Q: Can I print out my lists?

> **A:** Yes, there is a whole menu full of reports that you can print out.
>
> ◆   SoulMate Map©
>
> ◆   How Does Your Man Compare?
>
> ◆   Your B list = date topics
>
> ◆   Vacations, Goals and Retirement
>
> ◆   Red flag traits to avoid

Q: How do I ask you for coaching?

> **A:** You can write a comment at the bottom of any list.
>
> I am notified via email anytime someone writes a comment. I have the option to change the comment from private to public, or delete it after replying to you.
>
> I won't reply via the comment section unless a comment thread can contribute to others, instead I will send you a private email, informing you of the online coaching options. I'll delete any of your comments you don't agree to make public, after we've connected via email.
>
> You can also send me an email directly: askdenise@soulmateplan.com

Should You Do This Alone?

The final question you will want to answer is if you should you do this on your own or with help? That really depends on you. Do you prefer to work alone, or do you learn best when you can discuss with others? This workbook was actually compiled from the deeply refined process that I developed in my coaching sessions and exercises. I created this workbook because individual coaching can be expensive. This is a consolidated

Get Ready to Create Your SoulMate Map!

version, customized to guide any woman who wants to find her best match. However, if you feel like you could use an objective opinion throughout the process, you may be best off with help from someone who you know and can trust to be honest and up-front (rather than just telling you whatever you want to hear).

If you love the challenge and the experience of immersing yourself in a workbook on your own, great! I am sure you will do well. But, if you are not self-motivated or you don't like thinking out new concepts alone, then perhaps a group activity would be just your ticket. And for that, we offer a variety of group programs in conjunction with this workbook. (Note: We'll offer those opportunities, as they are available, via email. We promise not to become spammers and inundate you with unwanted marketing emails. We just want to be supportive and of service.)

While we are on the subject of ways to supplement your process, I should also let you know that if you are a SoulMate Plan member, there are free tele-seminars specifically for helping you through the last quarter of the SoulMate Map© process. If you need extra guidance sooner than that, or you aren't a member yet, then you can always join a tele-seminar series, our webinar series, or listen to a group of relationship experts discuss the chapters. There are all kinds of tools that we've made available to ensure your success, no matter how broad your learning needs might be. **You can find all this on our website SoulMatePlan.com**

Testimonials; from just a few of our clients:

"I was single for years. Just learning all of Denise's lessons made it possible for me to be more open. I am now happily in a committed relationship for 3 years now. Thank you, Denise."

❤

"The experience of dating again was enjoyable because I was clear about what I wanted in a way that was new for me. I know what I want; I know how to ask

for what I want. I know how to read men and help them to be great as a date. This new approach to dating was fun! I started out dating several guys so I would not limit myself. The result is I'm in love. I guess you could say, I was in the perfect mind set for the perfect guy to show up."

❤

"Within one week of opening my eyes to Denise's explanation about how to cultivate a man who is a "Diamond in the Rough" I met my future husband. I knew almost immediately he was the one!"

❤

I prefer to read and write on paper, so I was resistant to doing the exercises on-line. But I wanted the reports that are offered. So I called Denise and she gave me a quick lesson. I have to admit, the online was easy and fast. Plus the bonus of seeing suggested items to choose from truly made this a simpler and more profound method. To my great surprise, I learned a lot about myself in the process.

❤

Final Note: Once you've started, don't give up. It may be challenging, but when you finish the lessons, you will be **amazed by the different kinds of men that you will be attracted to** (and those that will be attracted to you)! Now let's get to it!

Chapter 9

How to Create Your Lists

Step 8: Create Your SoulMate Map© Lists

Now that we offer an online method to create your SoulMate Map©, below you will find instructions for both the online version and how to create your lists in a paper journal. The following chapters also offer inspiration and clarity about each of the lists of your SoulMate Map©.

Have fun!

This is the section you've been waiting for! Now you will finally uncover the right qualities you need in a partner! But be advised that this section will take time. It has been my experience throughout years of helping women come up with their lists that too much gets missed if you try to churn them all out in one sitting. So trust the process! Give each list the proper attention and thoroughness it deserves.

When you start on your first list, just open your journal and start free writing anything than comes to mind. Don't filter your thoughts and don't worry if it's right or wrong. You will have an opportunity at Step 9: "Grading Your SoulMate Lists" to weed out anything that really doesn't matter. Just give yourself the freedom to write anything down. The experience in the online version is different than journaling. On-line you will see a list of suggestions in the right column that others have come up with while creating their SoulMate Map©. They are there for you to either borrow the ideas of others, or inspire thoughts of your own.

Yes it works! So don't jump ahead; do it exactly in the order presented.

For some of you, this will be easy. For others, it will be confronting. If you fit into the latter category, don't do it alone. Engage in a conversation with someone who is analytical by nature and will help you kick-start your own thoughts on the subjects below.

There are several lists, all designed to help you unlock the truth and get you ready to turn your lists into your SoulMate Map©. Short changing your lists will lead to another broken picker, so make sure you embrace freedom, clarity and honesty as you work on them.

I imagine you may have made lists in the past, in your mind if not on paper. The importance of making written lists is that you are creating a new level of consciousness about the items on them. Remember the dream board? By writing these things down, you will finally manifest your intention of discovering the perfect partner for you, and that makes you much more likely to bring your A-game. If you have list items in your mind, you have already reached one level of awareness. If you write it down, you will experience a deeper level of intent to further your cause. Further down that path, if you share your lists with others, you will then be voicing these characteristics to a potentially active group of helpers (who will now know exactly what kind of guy would be a great hook up!)

Reviewing your lists will also intensify your awareness, and is essential to the process of creating your SoulMate Map©. Don't cut corners on this step. A weak list will create a weak map, and possibly lead you right back to where you started: Choosing men for the wrong reasons, and finding out the hard way that they were a mistake for you.

Unconsciously, you already have lists. For instance, perhaps you ended a failed relationship where the guy turned out to be narcissistic. He spent all his time working out. So mentally you said to yourself, I will never go out with a guy who is excessively interested in building his muscles. Or perhaps you go out with a guy who is cheap, and you have a new rule that you will never go out with a guy who doesn't tip, because you've determined that tipping is one of your signals to determine if a person has the same social consciousness as you. Those discoveries should not be ignored. Experience can be a good teacher.

Great! Now we need to take these rules that you created in your mind and turn them into great lists! Don't spend too much time analyzing your lists at this point. That comes later when we grade your map. As I mentioned earlier, this is the time where you just let the information flow, almost like brainstorming. The following exercise is designed to help you expand your lists.

Keep up with your list writing! You will think of a new one either every day or every other day, depending on the complexity of the list. Keep them all in your journal.

Step 8 Assignment

For Journalers:

Get a journal! All the list making will be entered in your journal. So choose one that you really love. After all, it's *your* love mate you are designing.

Your journal should be separate from the book for two reasons.

1) It's easy to expand as you grow. Who can predict how many entries you will enter in your list? You want to make sure you allow plenty of room for expansion. You might be adding to your lists for years to come.

2) It is easy to consult later. Your SoulMate Map© is a collection of ten lists that you can use from now on as your soul mate selection handbook. You'll want

to consult it frequently. Perhaps enough to be able to keep in your handbag. ❤

Get your journal ready! It's possible you might want to start with a notebook, and then transfer the fine-tuned list to a pretty journal, after you finished Step 9.

Whatever you do, don't limit your space for adding to your list later on. The better job you do on your lists the better chances you have of really discovering your perfect match.

For Online SoulMate Map:

Sign up for the on-line SoulMate Online Workbook. It's simple. Simply use the link below and create a user name and password to get started.

Copy this URL into your internet browser:

https://SoulMateMap.com/workbook

Chapter 10
What to Avoid in a Partner

List 1: Defining Your "Red" Flag List

If you are someone who wants to move forward and not repeat relationship mistakes, you don't have to look far to identify the red flags you learned from your past relationships. The opportunity here is to benefit from those lessons! If you fail to identify the red flags, then you will probably repeat the same mistakes. Therefore, we're starting with the red flags, so we can make lemonade out of your relationship lemons.

Look back on your past relationships and think hard on what did not work for you. Come up with a list of traits, qualities or situations that you want to avoid in your new model for a great relationship.

This is where you get to own the concerns that you have, based on your life's experiences, and the men you have dated or been with in a relationship. They could be traits you want to avoid in a man. They could be fears you have in life, or lifestyles you don't want with a partner.

Be truthful, after all... You want to find Your Match, not someone that will end in breakup.

So what if you are a glass is half empty person? To find a great match, you will want someone who does not make you feel like this quality is wrong. Or maybe you feel that by having your mate be the opposite, he will keep you in check. It helps if you know what is good for you. Here is a rule to help you decide: If you tend to be really interested in self-improvement articles, courses and studies, then you are a person who wants to change. If you thrive on change and

99

self-improvement, then you want someone who has the qualities you aspire to have. However, if you don't like change, if you feel that you are what you are or feel it's offensive to be with someone who wants to change himself, or even you, then make sure your list reflects that by writing down the attributes that you feel strongly about, even if they don't seem to have a positive slant on them.

List 1 instructions

While Online:

Create your list , by clicking on the **Defining Your "Red" Flags** bar.

I'll add some additional instruction at this point that apply to all online instructions:

- Don't worry about grading this list until you finish all the steps, then proceed to the "Grade your lists" section.

- The online process helps you to stay on track by not allowing you to go to the next list until you've completed the current list.

- Don't worry too much about getting your lists exactly right. You will always be able to go back and edit and/or add new items to your lists.

For Journalers:

In your journal, divide the page into four columns (use the example on the next page).

Enter the "bothersome traits" as short statements, not paragraphs. Perhaps putting this in a spreadsheet will become useful, since you will have the flexibility to make changes. However, a written list may be more visually effective for you, so it's your choice. Just keep in mind the format for List 2 on will be different. See the layout example below. Enter the list items in column A, with column B, C and D used to place an "x" in each column based on the following grade.

Column A = **Bothersome trait** - the trait that you know is problematic for you.

Column B = **I can handle** - it doesn't bother me too much; I can live with it.

Column C = **Want to see change** - frequently bothers me; I definitely want us to work together on eliminating this from our life.

Column D = **Deal breaker** – I won't tolerate this in my life, even a little!

Below, you will find examples on how to adapt constructively by using the cautions you have discovered. This will help guide your choices. If you get stuck, think about what areas you feel strongly about within these categories: Money, health, time management, social interactions, family interactions, public behavior, social skills, political views, religion, spirituality, exercise, safety, domesticity, activities, emotions, genetics, aging, appearance, sexuality, intimacy, gender, dominance, habits, monogamy, crime, deception,

If you are still stuck on what to enter on this list, discuss with your best friends what concerns *they* have. Maybe they will come up with ideas that will remind you of what matters to you. If that does not work, hop on a search engine and do some research.

Your chart should look something like this:

Bothersome trait	I can handle	Want to see change	Deal breaker!
Eats chips in bed	x		
Poor hygiene		x	
Has extra-marital affairs			x

Again, don't worry what other people will think, including me! No one is going to see this list but you. Don't lie to yourself, your future happiness in a relationship depends on your sincerity now!

List 2: Turning Mistakes into New Standards

Now that you have gotten the negative thoughts written down, let's use those red flags to identify positive traits you'd rather see in your mate. Simply look at each red flag trait and come up with a positive trait that would offset, or prevent you from falling for someone with that negative trait again.

List 2 Instructions

While Online:

Create your list by clicking on the **"Turning Mistakes into New Standards"** bar:

For Journalers:

Below your lists of red flags, create two columns. In the left column write all your red flags again, in the right column, come up with new standards that are the opposite of the red flags trait.

Here are some examples to help you complete this list.

Red flag	New Standard
Angry or abusive	Self control; respectful
Liar	Honest
Bad family relations	Loves his family and mine
Cheater	Loyal; Monogamous

Chapter 11

Your Happiness Lists

List 3: What Makes You HAPPY!

As I stated earlier, the greatest gift you can give to a man is your happiness. Therefore it's essential to know what makes you happy, or what gives you pleasure. Nothing is yummier or more fun for a man than to be around a woman who is experiencing her pleasure.

Now if you are a bit tired of making lists at this point, let me give you some motivation to help you re-energize yourself. You don't want to hold back with this list! Not only will it give you answers to your date's questions about what you want to do, but it's important to choose a relationship that will most definitely fulfill your happiness! Remember, this list is not a license to be a demanding diva princess in your relationship, but if you are not guiding your man to win at helping your happiness blossom, then the alternative is to become a woman who is either a suppressed martyr, or worse, a frustrated nag.

> "Happiness is the secret to inspiring a man's devotion and faithfulness!"

So really explore this list fully! If it's not natural for you to focus on your own happiness because of some attitude you picked up from your family during your upbringing, (like, "It's not nice or polite to focus on yourself,") then I have to tell you, that was something they told a child. You are now an adult, and as an adult, you need to learn the value of your happiness as the foundation for joyful and successful partnerships. All work and no play makes for a dull marriage too!

If you can only come up with ten things that make you happy, then you really need to take a notebook around with you regularly and jot down any ideas as they occur to you.

List 3 Instructions

Online:

Create your list by clicking on the **"What Makes You Happy"** bar.

Journalers:

Now create a **new, separate list** in your journal or spreadsheet, because all the lists from now on will use this new set of columns. From this list to list 10, you will only need to worry about the far left column. Enter one trait per line, because later on, you will grade them.

This list should look something like this:

Traits:	(leave blank for now)	(leave blank for now)	(leave blank for now)
Spending time together			
Massages			
Travel			

Here are some examples:
- I love to watch a sunset
- I love to be romanced
- I love having a husband who likes to play with his grandchildren
- I love the hours we spend talking about current events
- I love cuddling on the couch watching TV together.
- I love great conversations

List 4: What You Admire in People

Now create a list of the qualities you admire in people! Make it personal. Don't list what you think others will approve of. No one is going to see this list but you, so don't pollute the list with qualities you are trying to impress others with. For instance, if you admire Lance Armstrong because he has won the Tour de France several times, but you have no interests in biking or competitive sports, or marrying a man who has that commitment, it would not be a constructive choice for your lists! Choose qualities that matter to you!

Also include what you admire in your parent's marriage, or anyone else's relationship you admire.

A phrase you can use to help you with this list starts with: "I value..."

Another phrase is: "I am jealous of people who..."
Another phrase is: "I wish I had Jane Doe's ability to..."

List 4 Instructions

Online:

Create your list by clicking on the **"What You Admire in People" bar.**

Journalers:

Remember, enter one trait per line, because later on, you will grade them.
This list should look something like this:

Traits I Admire	(leave blank for now)	(leave blank for now)	(leave blank for now)
helpful			
ambitious			
peaceful			

You Have Great Qualities Too!

List 5: Your Qualities

A thorough and honest understanding of our own nature is important. Sometimes we take ourselves for granted. Or we can't even articulate what is great about ourselves! That stops now! Take the time to really explore what qualities you possess that are important to you. After all, how can you coordinate with his qualities if you are not aware of your own? Examples of your qualities and traits would be like the following:

Thrifty, resourceful, helpful, caring, inventive, sympathetic, empathetic, compassionate, great cook, adventurous, great communicator.

List 5 Instructions

Online:

Create your list by clicking on the **"Your Qualities"** bar.

Journalers:

Remember, enter one trait per line, because later on, you will grade them. Provide extra space after you've completed each list, so you can add to it when new thoughts occur. You may not think of everything all in one go.

My Qualities	(leave blank for now)	(leave blank for now)	(leave blank for now)
Happy			
Enthusiastic			
Organized			

If you need help, you can look at the lists found on this website <u>Human Traits List.</u>
(<u>http://www.gurusoftware.com/gurunet/personal/factors.htm</u>)

To help you get started, ask yourself these questions:

Examples:

"The great thing about me is that I am..."

"What I contribute to a relationship is..."

funny
clever
a glass half full person

Write down as many as you come up with! If you only come up with 10, think harder! You have more going for you than that! Don't short change yourself or the process!

List 6: Expressing Love

Not everyone expresses love and knows they are loved the same way. A mismatch on how you express and display your feelings, or how you recognize you are loved, can really lead to some dicey conversations, let alone hurt feelings.

For instance, if you don't like public displays of affection, and your guy grabs and smooches you in public, you will push him away and he will feel rejected. Or perhaps the reverse is true, and you will feel like the rejected one.

What if you like to cuddle on the couch while watching TV as a way of connecting or for quality intimate time, and he does not like to watch TV, or vice versa.

What if you like to hug or kiss and he does not?!

What if you like to spoon and he does not?!

I think you get my point. A disconnect in the way you express love, or in the way you feel loved, can lead to feelings of rejection and ultimately ruin the intimacy in the relationship. Keeping the flames and feelings alive in a relationship takes work, therefore it's valuable to have a mate that is compatible in the way they express and feel love.

List 6 Instructions

Online:

Create your list by clicking on the **"Expressing Love"** bar.

Journalers:

Create a new list called **"Expressing Love"**. Continue to list them the same way. Remember, enter one trait per line, because later on, you will grade them.

Here is a list of topics to help you come up with your list.

- How do you express love in public?

- How do you express love in private?

- How do you express love sexually?

- Do you have any feelings about the frequency of sex?

- How to you express your appreciation or acknowledgment?

- Do you prefer to show your love through words, actions or physically?

- What actions by your partner tells you he loves you?

- How are you about your space?

- How do you like to sleep with a mate?

- How important is gift giving to you?

- Is the frequency of time together important

Be mindful that generally speaking, men express love differently than you do, so when you grade this list later on, you will have a chance to determine which of these love expressions are a preference and which are a non negotiable.

Chapter 12

Want to Grow Old Together?

List 7: Lifestyle, Activities, Fun and Pursuits

Finally something light and fun! Make a list of the activities that you *currently* enjoy, and the ones you really want to do in the *future*. Don't add things that you would only want to do once or twice. For instance, if you want to have the experience of jumping out of a plane, but once is enough for you, then don't put it on your list.

Choose ongoing activities that you want to sustain throughout your life (at least that you are aware of for now). For instance, I can bowl and am willing to do it to be social, but it's not an activity I really like, so I wouldn't put it on my list. Don't you think it would be great to find someone who shares day-in and day-out activities? But don't worry if he does not match all your activity interests. It's also important to know this stuff so when he asks you what you want to do for fun, you are ready with an answer; something to offer besides, "I don't know, whatever you want to do."

> Side Benefit: Thinking about activities you enjoy will make it easier for a man, when he asks "What would you like to do".

For example, I love to go to arts and crafts festivals. It's one of my favorite things to do! Do you think my husband matches me in this interest? Heck no! But he loves taking me, because he gets a lot of pleasure out of watching me enjoy myself. Do you ever notice the guy that stands around while his woman takes time to explore each booth? Do you wonder why he does it? Because he is an awake man, and knows that it's important for him to accompany his wife when it's important to her. Your secret is to find his comfortable limits so he'll want to continue to go with you, and make it fun for him too. When my husband comes with me, he gets to have good food and drinks, and occasionally, there is one where they have a classic car show for him to enjoy. But what's most important is that your man feels good about your enjoyment and proud to be the man who provided it! Happy Wife, Happy Life!

So don't short change yourself! What do you authentically like to do?

List 8: Vacations

Since this is so closely related, you might as well add vacations to your list. The vacation list does not have to be long. However, for some people, travel is very important. So dream away!

It's good to be compatible in the area of vacations. Can you imagine what a nightmare it would be to spend the rest of your life wanting to simply read and relax by a pool while your significant other relentlessly pursues thrill-seeking on his vacation? He wants an adrenaline rush vacation and you want a way to decompress and relax, or visa-versa.

List 7 & 8 Instructions

Online:

Create your list by clicking on the corresponding bars.

Journalers:

Continue by adding these lists to your journal or spreadsheet.

List 7:   Activities Instructions

For each line, add an activity that you truly enjoy doing! Remember, this is not a public, online dating profile. It's the true, honest, unbridled list of what you enjoy, whether it's gardening and watching TV, or hiking and dancing salsa. Once again, don't short-change yourself! Writing this list might seem simple and obvious to you now, but later on, it will probably have a much more profound impact than you expect!

List 8:   Vacations Instructions

The vacation list does not have to be long, but it certainly can be if you want it to be! Don't restrain yourself or be bogged down by realism. Just list the types of vacations you would like to experience, including the kind that is still just a pipe dream at this point, but remains a true ambition of yours. Also list the types of activities you like to do on vacations. If you used to like to Jet Ski, but now you have back problems that prevent that, don't add it to your list. Add the activities that you not only want to, but can participate in. You don't need to list every place you want to visit. Instead, make categories such as domestic travel, beach vacations, adventurous trips, or vehicle-only travel if you don't want to get on a plane.

However, if there are destinations that are special to you, add them! It's your list.

List 9:   Goals, Retirement, Education and Growth

Goals are important factors in compatibility, so don't take this exercise for granted! Goals can be about finances, about how you want to live your senior years, what achievements you want to obtain in life.

If you have specific goals for retirement, write them down. Can you imagine what a strain it would be on the relationship if one person wants to plan for retirement, while the other is living in the now and thinks it will all work out somehow? The person wanting to plan will resent the one refusing to look ahead, and vice versa.

If pursuits of higher education are important, you probably won't be compatible with a person who believes in the road of hard knocks as the best education. You may even find that his lack of education diminishes your respect for him, because a good education is part of a standard you have set in your mind. Don't get me wrong. I am not suggesting that any of these attitudes in life are the norm. They are just random suggestions. The point is to explore the goals that strongly affect your mindset ahead of time, and figure them out before you find yourself in a relationship with someone with conflicting ambitions!

Ever hear people say they broke up because they grew apart? Wouldn't it be nice to know if your future life partner shares your feelings about growth and learning? What if you have ambitions to go back to college and achieve the degree you always dreamed of, but he thinks it's a waste of time? Or you enjoy self-help programs and he thinks they are silly? Don't you think that, over time these will become a wedge in your relationship? He may be fun to be with now, but later on, when you discover he is not interested in growth or change, while you are all about it, your relationship will face a huge challenge. Likewise, if you don't have any ambitions for learning and growth, you don't want to be with a man for whom those things are a primary focus. He'll go pursue his evolution, and you will have nothing left to talk about. Your ability to relate to each other can collapse this way. Perhaps you will have the kind of relationship that allows for each other's growth or pursuits without losing the connection to the partnership. In any case, writing it down is important. At the very least, it's something worth discussing before you walk down the aisle. Write down your intentions for these issues, and include the area of spirituality in your list, because the pursuit of spiritual growth or lack thereof is an important factor in compatibility.

List 9 Instructions

Online:

Create your list by clicking on the **"Goals, Retirement, Education and Growth"** bar.

Journalers:

Continue by adding these lists to your journal or spreadsheet.

What do to...

What are your goals for the future? Separate your list into achievable goals and lofty goals.

List your goals about finances, family, vacations, home life, possessions, purchases, health, fitness, lifestyle, work, community, status, achievements, education, etc.

List the areas where you want to learn. What subjects, degrees, certifications, ongoing studies do you want to pursue? For example, they could be something you would achieve through an institution, programs offered by experts, or online pursuits. They could be based on spirituality, self-improvement, finances or health; consider these list items as a place-holder for what you would like to pursue someday.

Keep up the good work! Don't lose steam now! You are about half way done with the list portion of the workbook.

List 10: Physical Attraction

I'm adding physical attributes to your lists against my better judgment. But it's a sticking point for some of you, so I might as well include it. However, I'll give you a tip right now: To focus on a man's physical appearance as your primary guideline is definitely a broken picker!

I know a guy who has declared, "She must have green eyes." He is still single. Surprise, surprise! When you focus on superficial qualities, you get superficial results! It's amazing how many people are surprised by this. That being said, attraction has its value, so go ahead and make your list of qualities that you find attractive. Get it out of your system and don't censor yourself. It does not matter what you write now. Later on, when you create your SoulMate Map©, you will have the opportunity to put these qualities in perspective. So for now, have fun with it. If it's not that important, don't make stuff up! You're already ahead of the curve.

List 10 Instructions

Online:

Create your list by clicking on the **"Physical Attributes"** bar.

Journalers:

Continue by adding these lists to your journal or spreadsheet.

That Was Your Final List!

However, this isn't over yet. The fun is just beginning! The next step is to refine your lists, to ultimately reveal your A List! In fact, just doing the homework will raise your bar!

You are welcome to add to your lists now as ideas pop into your head. Hopefully you left some extra space as mentioned earlier.

Chapter 13

Your Soul Mate Finally Revealed

Step 9: Grading Your SoulMate Map© Lists

Get ready for this is the culmination of everything you've built so far, and the final process where you will create the final product that you have been patiently working towards: Your SoulMate Map©!

First, read the guidelines below. Once you understand the guidelines, go to your lists either online or on paper, and start grading.

Refresher - These are the topics of the lists you have defined so far:

Qualities, Traits and Interests:
> List 1 – Red-flags
> List 2 – Turn Mistakes into New Standards
> List 3 – What Makes You Happy
> List 4 – What You Admire in People
> List 5 – Your Qualities
> List 6 – Expressing Love
> List 7 – Lifestyle, Activities, Fun Pursuits
> List 8 – Vacations
> List 9 – Goals, Retirement, Education and Growth
> List 10 – Physical Attributes

Now, we are going to rate all the qualities and values you want in a mate! Remember those empty columns to the right of your list items? Here, we will rate each quality and trait by how important it is to you. You are going to rate A, B, or C, where A's are deal-breakers, B's make you happy and are nice little bonuses, and C's are are no longer a necessity for a healthy relationship.

The rating process is very important. In fact, many women have had epiphanies while doing this part of the exercise. You may have found the process of list creation alone to be illuminating, but when you really have to put a pen to grade it, you will discover how you have betrayed your own values and needs all these years without even knowing it.

> Rating System:
> A = Must Have
> B = Important but not deal breaker
> C = Not important

Don't struggle, and remember you can tweak your ratings as you become more aware of your feelings and experiences.

Here are the guidelines for how to grade your lists:

The first one is for ranking the importance of every entry you put into your list, as follows:

A = Must Have! Non-negotiable!

Look at your list, and for each entry that you passionately consider a quality or trait that you MUST have in a partner, mark it with an A. By down-playing the importance of "A" qualities, so as not to rule any men out, you will only perpetuate the lowering of your bar. So be fair, and be honest!

If your list is predominately "A"s, then look again and realize that you are choosing traits you will not negotiate on. He must have these or no deal! An example of a trait that could seem like an "A", but is in fact a "B" is "Patient listening skill". The question to ask yourself is whether this is a character trait that you can't live with or can't live without?

B = Nice to Have, But if He Doesn't, I Want Him to at Least Recognize How Important This is to Me!

"B" traits are a definite plus, and they're important, but can you accept it if he could develop this later? Let's use the example of "Patient listening skills". This would be a "B", unless you had an abusive situation growing up and you feel traumatized when someone interrupts you while you are talking, which makes it completely intolerable for you.

The other definition of a "B" is that the trait or interest is something that you value highly, and while you don't need him to possess it or engage in it, you want him to honor, respect and support you, because it's essential to your happiness. An example might be that you love to dance. Dancing brings you joy and you wish your man would join you. But because he does not, it does not mean you would break up with him. Instead, you want him to support you or encourage you to go dancing with friends. He appreciates that dancing is something special to you. Therefore, if the quality, activity or trait is really important to you, but he doesn't have to be it, or like it himself, mark it as a "B".

C = Not Important.

Just kidding! It really represents what you could very comfortably live without in the big scheme of things. It would be like more of a "luxury" than a "need".

Example: you enter "salsa dancing" on your list. You enjoy salsa dancing, but it does not qualify as a "B" because it's not essential to your happiness. In fact, it feels more like a nice to have, than a must have. Therefore rate it a "C", unless you are looking for a relationship with someone who will also be your competitive partner on the salsa dancing circuit. "C" tends to be more frivolous or superficial in nature. They are fun to add to the list, but you certainly are not going to end a relationship over them!

Think of it this way...

If all of your lists were about a home instead of a man, then the A's are the qualities that are critical, like location, foundation and structure. The B list is what makes you smile and gives pleasure to your heart, like a nice fireplace or garden. The C's are throw away wishes. It's nice to wish for them, but in the greater scheme of life, they were unrealistic to begin with. For example, you might like spiral staircases, but you can't allow that to influence your decision.

Here is an example of how to use your spreadsheet; it should look something like this:

What you admire	Rate A= Must Have B= Nice to Have C= Not Important	leave blank for rating your mate later.
Patient listening skills		
Handy around the house		
Cooks		
Similar sense of humor		

This is Your SoulMate Map©

Now that you have painstakingly identified which qualities and traits matter to you, and you have tagged each one for their importance, you know what kind of man you are looking for.

Step 9 Assignment

While Online:

If you chose to create your SoulMate Map© online and you have completed your lists, you can click on the grading menu bar to see a page with all the lists you created thus far, that can be graded. Follow the guidelines below to grade them. By clicking on each list's menu bar, it should be obvious how to proceed.

For Journalers:

Let's begin integrating your lists into your map. Every list you have created so far (except the red flag list) should all be graded and the A's collected into one list. The final A list is your SoulMate Map©. (Hopefully you have been expanding your lists as new items popped into your mind.)

If you have not done so already, go through your lists, and line by line, rate each element either an A, B, or C

Give this slow and careful consideration, and be willing to change your grades as any new awareness reveals itself!

Chapter 14

How Do Men in Your Past Rate

Step 10: Compare Your Men to Your Lists

This step will really help you to see where you have wasted your time on past or current relationships. For my clients who were hopelessly stuck on the wrong guy before they created their SoulMate Map©, the truth was starkly clear by the time they were finished with the process. In fact, many were pretty flabbergasted about how obvious their incompatibilities suddenly were. Sometimes we ourselves can't see when a person isn't good for us, because we are blinded by love, or what we think is love.

Your SoulMate Map© will help you to see where the bumps will be, and recognize whether you are truly compatible in the areas that most people don't analyze when falling in love. The big opportunity that the SoulMate Map© provides is the ability to use a reliable framework that illuminates the areas that most people are blind to when they leap into their relationships.

Use the SoulMate Map© as a guideline to help you recognize whether your man has the important qualities you want and need. **However, don't use the SoulMate Map© for analysis paralysis!** In other words, don't turn your map into an opportunity to obsess over imperfections in a date, and therefore eliminate every man as a possible mate. Don't expect to find someone who fills your list 100% and don't ignore areas of possible growth. Lastly, don't suddenly whip this out in front of a guy and then grade him right there on the spot!

Use This Like a Normal Map:

If he fails on most of the must-haves on your A list, then is it time to stay or go back to the dating market?

If you find a guy who has some of the key must haves, then maybe he's worth your time, and you should help guide him to success.

The SoulMate Map© could help you to see where you have been too critically focused on the trivial "C" qualities of someone instead of looking at how compatible they are on the A and B lists, ensuring you never gave a chance to the diamonds in the rough!

True Story:

When I met my dream husband, I had an instant dislike to the way he looked! I wasn't attracted to him physically. He drove a minivan, which to me was a flag for being a soccer dad (I was beyond the age of wanting young children in my life), and he personified the term "dork". (If you knew my husband, then you would understand that this is not only an accurate characterization, but one that his whole family finds endearing about him!) Anyway, I instantly cast him off as NOT boyfriend material. You could say, I cared more about the C traits and was yet to know whether he had any of my A traits.

Even though I was not interested, he insisted on wooing me. I still wasn't interested, but I allowed him into my life as a friend. Thank goodness, because if I had followed the strategy of not even allowing him to be a friend, I would have missed out on the love of my life.

Eventually I saw the diamond in the rough that was there. I was judging him on the superficial traits of a man: his looks and whether he represented the image of the kind of guy that I "saw myself with". I did not have a SoulMate Map© at the time. It did not exist. So I was just as guilty as most of the women out there for ignoring and taking the really good guys for granted while wasting my time on the charmers!

Here is what turned the corner for me. I discovered I could have in-depth conversations with him, which is very important to me. Over time, I found that I loved talking to him, and we could have conversations that I could not have with most people. He had never given up his efforts to win my affection, so one day, I agreed to a date, even though we lived in different states. He was clearly and openly into me and was going to great lengths to keep me interested. Through our conversations, I discovered his values were the same as mine. His passions were mostly in line with mine, and we had the ability to discuss difficult issues. I felt so safe with him. He passed on the essential "Man In Love" test, which I am hoping (by this point in the workbook) you know means: **He was devoted to learning what makes me happy.**

> I could have missed out on the greatest husband if I stuck with my old criteria for choosing a mate.

So one day, I had a deep conversation about what I wanted in a partner. He not only listened, he listened well, and more importantly, he was willing to have the conversation (how many men do you know who will do that?) I gave him my declaration of what I wasn't willing to compromise on. I could tell he really took it seriously and then in turn, with a powerful confidence, he declared how he could be that man. Next, I diplomatically, and artfully, expressed my concerns about him. Then he showed me his true substance of character, because instead of acquiescing he stood his ground and explained his nature in a way that revealed a whole new side of him that I had been missing until that point. Wow! He impressed me in so many ways throughout this process! Having the guts to hold this conversation helped me to see a new side of him that I found sexy; particularly his integrity and his unyielding devotion to my happiness, especially because that devotion came with healthy boundaries for his well-being and dignity. I knew he would never allow himself to become some love sick guy that would compromise who he was for love, and I respected him all the more for it!

While I didn't have a SoulMate Map© back then, I did have a list, although it was much less comprehensive. I found that he actually did fit all the big points that would have been on my A list.

Now for the areas that are "nice to have," or "inconsequential," qualities, I hated the way he dressed! There. I said it. I admit I was superficial! But here is the amazing part. One day, long before we had the serious talk, while we were still in the courting stage, he wanted to take me out shopping (his guy way of impressing me). I told him I was not comfortable with us shopping for me, and suggested instead that we shop for him. I admit, I was a bit uncomfortable picking out shirts and pants for him. But he was so eager to look like the man I would find attractive, it turned out to be a fun experience. Plus, it showed me a glimpse into what life would look like with him. The best part is that I discovered a whole new attraction for him. With his new look, I thought he looked great! Suddenly the barrier of not being attracted to him was gone!

As I've mentioned before, our past mistakes are often the best teachers. I recommend that you run your *old* boyfriends through your new map to get clear on what you really want. Perhaps this will help you to tweak your SoulMate Map©, or maybe it will give you some perspective, and the answers you have always been seeking.

> Rate your past men against your new SoulMate Map. Perhaps you will discover he didn't come close, or maybe he was missing a majority of the "must haves".

Step 10 Assignment

While Online:

Click on the Menu bar: **"Grade Your Men"**

There are three columns, for up to three former relationships (or even future relationships), for you to compare to your list. All the A qualities are collected on this one page for you to find out how your man compares. As you select each matching item the score will float near the top of the screen.

For Journalers:

You finally get to fill in column 3! Enter an old boyfriend's name at the top of Column 3. You can use columns 4, 5, and so on to add more ex's.

Now go down the list and simply place a check in the column under his name of the attributes, values and traits that you feel he really possessed. Not like, "Yeah, he did that once," or, "I think he would have if the opportunity had presented itself."

Observe your thought process while you check or don't check his traits. Are you being really lenient because you want him to pass? Are you being super critical because you are really angry with him? Do you find yourself making excuses for his missing traits? This should tell you things about yourself that will be handy to keep in mind when you do the same for a new love interest.

Use these questions to help you get a new perspective about him:

1. Did he score high or low?
2. Can you see now that there is no way he could have been a suitable partner for you?
3. Did he score high in one or two areas, and you

built a sense of love and attachment on just a few good qualities?

4. How would life have been if you had stayed with a man that did not offer you most of the traits you need in a partner?

In your journal, list the steps you are willing to take now to become free from these issues.

The Best Part of This Exercise

After you finished checking down your ex's list of attributes, look at what traits he had that you felt were your must-haves from your A list. How many did he have? Did he have most of them? Did he have only two?

Seeing how your ex performed on this list should be a wake-up call to you. Often, we fall in love with one or two endearing traits that are really special, and we build an entire love affair with this man over those two traits. I have to repeat, so you don't miss it: I can't begin to tell you how important it is for you to think hard about whether that is true of your relationships. Have you built an entire love affair around the one or two special traits that he has? Can you see now that the other 49+ traits that he is missing explains why you are in love, yet so miserable?

Do you hang in there and want to give him chance after chance because of the feelings that you once had when you fell you in love with him over those two traits? And every time he reveals

> A friend of mine ignored her SoulMate Map and married her fiancé who failed most of the qualities on her list. They had a tumultuous marriage that ended badly.

those two special traits, you probably find yourself falling for them all over again, because they have a magic power over you!

Now that you can see what is truly important to you in a partner and a soul mate, it should be clear how you were blinded in the past to the inequity that he brought to your life and to what he failed to "be". Maybe now, you can stop fantasizing about the what ifs. He either had it or he didn't, and wasting a life waiting for him to have it is a shame.

Whenever I give this test to women and they see that, one, he really wasn't anywhere near the man she really wants, and two, that she had an illusion about the man she had been painfully in love with for years, a wake-up occurs. There it is, in black and white. No more excuses, just the truth. For the first time, the fog lifts and the clear reality settles in. When you can see it that way, the spell is broken and you can more easily move on with your life!

And what if your ex had most of the traits you were looking for, and the relationship still failed? Well, without interviewing both of you, it's hard to say. It could be a few things. Maybe, you were not a match on his list. However, if you were really honest with yourself and thorough with your lists, and he fulfilled most of your needs, then he has to have been missing the desire to make you happy. Otherwise you would still be together.

If you are still stuck after the following exercise and just can't let him go, then I suggest you either hire a professional therapist or check out our website for programs designed to enhance your love education.

To find these quick coaching programs, go to our website: http://SoulMatePlan.com

Chapter 15

Please Pay it Forward

I am on a mission to raise the awareness of women and to empower them to make better choices and to choose a healthier love. So if you feel someone else can benefit from this series, please recommend they start it for themselves. I *hope you honor my efforts by suggesting they buy the book and sign-up for the online SoulMate Map© Workshop, so they not only experience it the way you did*, but also to support my efforts in spreading this wonderful knowledge. And of course, encouraging your friends to make this investment is the greatest compliment you could ever send! After all, friends only recommend the wisest investments to friends, so that's how I will know that an impact has truly been made in your life.

I love providing guidance and hope to contribute to your growth for many years. Because even the greatest wake-up call won't last, it's important to refresh and reinforce what you've learned with reminders and repeated lessons. Even if it's something as simple as reading blog articles to keep it all fresh! So, promise yourself to keep this conversation alive and well in your life. Whether it is with SoulMate Plan, or Relationships 123 (a site devoted to teaching partnership lessons to couples, at http://relationships123.com) or with any other relationship expert that keeps your mind and your heart open.

Congratulations on finishing your SoulMate Map©

I don't want to lose touch with you, and I love receiving testimonials so I can share your success with other women who are struggling to find love! To share your SoulMate Map© experience, send an email to me at: Service@SoulMateMap.com. If you would like to keep up to date with the latest relationship research and information we discovered, you can subscribe to my online blog which will be sent to you via email once per month. All members will automatically receive emails notifying them of a new blog entry.

You've finished the SoulMate Map©, and that is an outstanding accomplishment, but there is still so much more to learn! Did you enjoy and benefit from reading your lessons and answering questions about yourself truthfully? **Has this book altered your understanding about men, love and relationships?** If the answer is a big lovely, happy YES, then you are among the special group of women who are ready to take their love education to a new level. After all, I couldn't pack everything I've learned into one book, and I'm still working hard to gather more invaluable knowledge for all women who believe the love of their dreams can become a reality!

Are you feeling like you are stumped, or you feel your lists are too sparse? We have a few teleseminars to help you out. Some are free, some are low cost, and some are only offered to members.

If you are really committed to improving your patterns, you might want to consider joining the SoulMate Plan email notifications. That is the best way to learn about any upcoming teleseminars or webinars.

If you want to continue your path to GREAT love, then check out all SoulMate Plan programs. They are designed to be affordable and allow you to work at your own pace. It's just like love college, you get to choose how many courses you want to study and whether you want to gain a master's degree or just start slow and take a self-study program.

Here they are:

SoulMate Plan's Free Offerings

Free Gift: (2 Products)
                   30 Days of Dating Tips
                   Eye-Opening Dating Lesson

Love Blog: Provocative love stories and tips.

Ready for the NEXT Level of Your Love Education?

SoulMatePlan.com Offers More Love Education:

Top Ten Relationships Skills Every Woman Should Know

Understanding Men

Raise Your Standards

Healthy Love Patterns

Selecting a Better Soul Mate

Being the Best Partner

Secret Powers of Women

Your Happiness

Online Dating Tips

Communication Skills

Letting Go

Want to Learn with an Expert?

SoulMate Plan offers a variety of products to help you learn:

Tele-seminars

Tele-seminar Series

Audio Lessons

Webinars

Private Groups

Of course you can also stay in touch with SoulMate Plan socially on Facebook:

www.Facebook.com/SoulMatePlan

Visit the website at http://SoulMatePlan.com.

I hope you have enjoyed these lessons. I hope it awakened you to the power and excitement that you embody as a woman. I hope it raised your bar and you have a new appreciation for what men want and how to choose a better mate.

I look forward to hearing your feedback on this series, on your experiences, and your inspired "aha" moments. If you feel your awakening will help to inspire other women, please share your thoughts via the testimonial or program review pages. If you bought via the website and provided your email, I will follow up with an email, offering you the opportunity to share your encouragements, so other women can read them on our site.

**Bless You! And Remember,
Love is Closer Than You Think**

The following pages were left blank for note taking

www.ingramcontent.com/pod-product-compliance
Lightning Source LLC
Chambersburg PA
CBHW070800290326
41931CB00011BA/2086